D0771718

THE
ATHEIST'S
FATAL
FLAW

THE
ATHEIST'S
FATAL
FLAW

EXPOSING CONFLICTING BELIEFS

NORMAN L. GEISLER AND
DANIEL J. McCOY

BakerBooks
a division of Baker Publishing Group
Grand Rapids, Michigan

Published by Baker Books
a division of Baker Publishing Group
P.O. Box 6287, Grand Rapids, MI 49516-6287
www.bakerbooks.com

Printed in the United States of America

Library of Congress Cataloging-in-Publication Data is on file at the Library of Congress, Washington, DC.

ISBN 978-0-8010-1646-2 (pbk.)

Scripture quotations are from The Holy Bible, English Standard Version® (ESV®), copyright © 2001 by Crossway, a publishing ministry of Good News Publishers. Used by permission. All rights reserved. ESV Text Edition: 2011

14 15 16 17 18 19 20   7 6 5 4 3 2 1

This book is affectionately dedicated to my faithful wife of over fifty years, whose excellent help has vastly improved this and numerous other manuscripts.

Norman Geisler

This book is dedicated to my beautiful wife. You are such a gift from God to me and to our daughters. Thank you for marrying me!

Daniel McCoy

Contents

Acknowledgments

We would like to thank the following people for their role in making this book possible:

Mark Hanna for his valuable insights

Scott Matscherz for his technical suggestions

Joseph Holden for his encouragement

Robert Hosack and the staff at Baker for seeing the potential in this project and seeing it through

Our families for their patience and love

Beth McCoy for the artwork on the contract

Introduction

Doublethink means the power of holding two contradictory beliefs in one's mind simultaneously, and accepting both of them.

—George Orwell, *Nineteen Eighty-Four*[1]

One night, my (Daniel's) three-year-old daughter, Beth, complained to my wife and me as we put her to bed: "I need a snack; my tummy is very full." My wife and I laughed at the contradiction. It was merely a semantic contradiction, fixable by tweaking the words. The aim of this book is the diagnosis of other, far more serious contradictions. If I had lectured my daughter about how her statement was a contradiction and about the perils of violating the laws of logic, she would all the while be thinking about snacks and wondering when I would stop talking so she could have some. In contrast, we hope to show that our diagnosis should not be ignored by the thinking atheist. Before proceeding, it will be helpful to define the terms that will be used in this diagnosis. In so doing, we set out in general terms the arguments we investigate in much more detail, and in the atheist's own words, in the chapters that follow.

1

God-in-the-Dock Arguments

The first term we define is *God-in-the-dock* (GITD) *argument*. We have taken the phrase from a C. S. Lewis essay,[2] and as an adjective *God-in-the-dock* will stand for the family of atheistic arguments that place God on trial for having contradicted his own nature. These arguments designate a particular action or inaction by God as incompatible with his perfect nature. We define his nature according to his infinite holiness, power, knowledge, and love. Each atheistic argument considered is a GITD argument, so each might be framed in such a way:

> If God were truly moral, he would not [action].
>
> God does [action].
>
> Thus, God is not truly moral.

Of course, if God is not truly moral, then a moral God does not exist. Thus, more pointedly, the infinitely moral God of Christianity does not exist. It is true that some of the arguments that follow can be construed in ways other than GITD. For example, one might say, "The kind of totalitarian submission called for by the Christian God is evidence that Christianity was concocted by opportunists." However, we are concerned with the version of the argument that says, for example, "If God were a truly loving God, he would not demand our submission."

Note that because these are GITD arguments, it is only fair to remain within the Christian framework throughout the critique. It is trickery to argue, for example, "It is immoral of God to judge us for 'sins,' since we were never sinners because there was never a God to sin against in the first place." No, if you are arguing that it is immoral of God to do such and such, then you must not caricature the Christian system to make it easier to knock down. If you want to argue against Christianity, let it be the real thing.

It is important to prevent this illicit caricaturing early in the game because of a tempting tactic that might arise throughout. The atheist who argues that God does not do enough to fix the problem of moral evil often claims that the kind of morality God foists on humankind is actually immoral and thus makes the problem of moral evil worse. We are told that this immoral morality includes nasty prescriptions to faith, worship, and so on to which no dignified human should stoop. Yet if God exists, are not such prescriptions perfectly understandable, even inevitable? You cannot ask God for a godless morality. This book will not venture outside of GITD arguments against the coherence of Christianity, with the agreement that the atheist will not hop the fence mid-argument to snatch, bring back, and sneak in caricatures.

The Atheist

Throughout the book, it will be common to read statements beginning with the subject *the atheist* or *the atheists*. Please understand we never intend to speak for all atheists. When we speak of "the atheist," we are merely referring to the atheist who holds the atheistic arguments under discussion. There may well be many atheists who do not hold to these particular arguments but instead disbelieve in God on the basis of other arguments. Similarly, we have used the generic "he" for ease of expression.

The Problem of Moral Evil

The third term in need of definition is the *problem of moral evil*. According to Richard Swinburne, "The main argument against the existence of God has always been the 'argument from evil'—that is, from pain and malevolence. . . . Evils are traditionally divided into moral evils (ones knowingly caused or allowed to occur by humans) and natural evils (the ones for which humans are not responsible, such as the effects of disease and earthquake)."[3] What Swinburne calls "moral evils" is what we have in mind as the problem of moral evil. As Philip Quinn puts it, "*Moral evil* inheres in the wicked actions of moral agents and the bad consequences they produce. An example is torturing the innocent. When evil actions are considered theologically as offenses against God, they are regarded as sins."[4]

Suppose the atheist recoils from such an incriminating definition of the problem of moral evil. Perhaps he disbelieves in moral agency and would loathe to call a fellow human wicked. Recall, however, our no-fence-hopping rule from the above discussion of GITD arguments. Because, according to Christianity, a free humanity is capable of misusing their freedom to commit horrendous wickedness, then to try to soften what is meant by moral evil will fall short of fairness. When the atheist advances the problem of moral evil as a GITD argument against the Christian God, he cannot step outside Christianity to define moral evil solely in terms of genetics. If God is on trial for being inconsistent in himself, it would be absurd of the jury to rule that he should be even more inconsistent. As long as the argument starts out, "If the Christian God were really . . . ," moral evil remains defined by Christianity as having arisen from human wickedness.

The Problem of Divine Intervention

Our fourth definition involves a second GITD argument. A second problem, just as oppressive as the problem of moral evil, confronts the atheist. God is no longer the absent deliverer as under the problem of moral evil; now God has arrived as the oppressor himself. The term to be defined here is the *problem of divine intervention*. Under the problem of moral evil, we find that God is not present enough, yet in this new problem we find God to be too present. In the same breath, the atheist utters "Please" followed by "No, thank you." According to the problem of divine intervention, the interventions the Christian God introduces into human life are immoral. Thus, by appealing to the argument, the atheist makes clear that he does not want or need these interventions.

The problem of divine intervention is really a family of arguments. There are ten allegedly immoral interventions we will examine throughout the book. The atheists we will consult demand freedom from God in the following ten areas. God should not

1. demand submission,
2. bestow favor,
3. authorize death,
4. require faith,
5. attach guilt,
6. prescribe rules,
7. administer punishment,
8. grant pardon,
9. send to hell,
10. bring to heaven.

Thus, the atheist who initially asked for God's intervention into the problem of moral evil does not, in the end, actually need him.

Three distinctions will help pinpoint what is meant when the atheist asks for "freedom from divine intervention." First, "I don't need God" is to be distinguished from similar declarations, such as, "I don't need God to explain the origin of life," or "I don't need God to explain where morality comes from." Such arguments, based on which is the better explanation, are not dealt with here. It is not God as a theoretical explanation that is in the dock here, but, in fact, God as himself. Second, we ought to distinguish between freedom from God's interventions and freedom from the religious establishment. One finds overlap, but much atheistic ink is used condemning Christian doctrines and actions that cannot be fairly traced back to the Founder of Christianity. What we have in mind in what follows is a call for freedom from the interventions of God himself, as described in the Old and New Testaments. Third, the idea of divine intervention sounds quite dramatic, but it ought to be kept in mind that none of these interventions are actually imposing enough as to overturn human freedom. As we see in the section "The Levels of Intervention" below, these interventions never involve the coercive manipulation of free will. Rather, these interventions should be taken as interventions that work on the willing conscience.

Human Autonomy

We have defined two GITD arguments against God's existence—namely, the problem of moral evil and the problem of divine intervention. It should not be difficult to see why the atheist sees moral evil as a problem. For one thing, no one could deny that moral evil causes vast amounts of suffering. However, why is the second argument called the *problem* of divine intervention? If the atheist truly sees moral evil as a problem, should not the atheist restate the latter argument as the *solution* of divine intervention? This might be if divine intervention did not threaten a cherished value atheists hold called *human autonomy*. Divine intervention diminishes human autonomy, and thus itself becomes a problem even while solving another.

The word *autonomy* literally means "self-law."[5] One can be ruled by self or by something outside the self, such as others or God. Thus theologian Paul Tillich categorized the hierarchy of rule as autonomy (rule by self), heteronomy (rule by another), and theonomy (rule by God). Tillich scholar Michael Palmer explains, "Autonomous reason is thus independent reason, reason refusing to obey any authority, be it secular or divine, which seeks to control the way it grasps or shapes reality."[6] Because divine intervention would naturally confront human autonomy and because, as we will see, most atheists seem to be zealots for autonomy, divine intervention would be seen as a problem. Now, whereas Christians and atheists alike appreciate being granted freedom (i.e., freedom to make personal choices), freedom is not identical to autonomy. True, personal freedom permits oneself to rule autonomously; freedom could even be seen to encourage autonomy if one sees God as an impediment to freedom. Yet freedom permits the reverse as well. Those who freely obey God often see themselves as freer when living out God's purposes than when they had enslaved themselves to various sins out from under his guidance.

The Levels of Intervention

Though many versions of the problem-of-evil argument suggest that God should intervene to prevent *all* cases of evil, suppose that an atheist backpedals and says, "Well, obviously, to get rid of all moral evil would obliterate human autonomy. I am not saying God should do anything as rash as that. I just think he should at least prevent the more horrendous evils, like child abuse and such." Because this distinction by degrees alters the argument, it will be helpful to propose a categorization. In descending order, let us propose three ways God could intervene in the problem of moral evil:

A ("All")—Forcible prevention of all moral evil

B ("Bad")—Forcible intervention into the most egregious cases of evil

C ("Conscience")—Voluntary intervention at the mental/spiritual level

The atheist who says, "God should fix everything," and then inserts, "But God shouldn't touch anything," is contradicting himself. However, if an atheist says, "I don't want God to fix everything, just the worst things," does that dissolve the contradiction? To answer, first, it must be clear what it is the atheist wants God not to touch. As we will see, the atheist wants freedom from God's interventions insofar as God commands things like faith, submission, and guilt, and insofar as God promises things like death, judgment, and afterlife. Although such interventions might seem restricting, they rely on *voluntary* responses. God might command, but man might refuse. God might promise, but one might distract oneself into forgetfulness. In other words, these commands and promises leave free will intact. No inch of autonomy is seized from the unwilling. Yet it is freedom from such voluntary interventions that the atheist demands. It is a demand for freedom from C-level interventions.

When the atheist says, "God should fix the problem of moral evil," which level is he requesting? There are two possibilities. The atheist to whom *all* moral evil should have been or should be prevented is asking for A-level intervention. It would seem that this would entail the abolition of true moral freedom. B-level intervention is represented by the statement, "I'm not saying God should get rid of all evil, but *at least* the worst cases of it." Yet how could God answer such a request practically? Either God designs the human up front without the ability to do significant damage, with built-in physical or mental constraints, much like chastity belts and training wheels. Or, if there be no constitutional constraints on human freedom, God intervenes at the moment prior to the urge or the act, so that, for example, as C. S. Lewis put it, "a wooden beam became soft as grass when it was used as a weapon, and the air refused to obey me if I attempted to set up in it the sound waves that carry lies or insults."[7] So the request is for either A- or B-level interventions. He could not be arguing in favor of mere C-level interventions, for, if that were the case, there would be no argument, since those types of interventions are precisely what Christianity offers. In dropping his request from A-level down to B-level interventions, the atheist is still asking God to move mountains: erasing a near infinity of free actions either at creation or throughout history through literally countless miracles.

As we will discover in the section on the problem of divine intervention, the atheist sees it as immoral of God to intervene at the C level. Yet when it comes to the problem of moral evil, the atheist demands God to intervene at either A level or B level. Admittedly, it sounds extreme to accuse the atheist of wanting God to fix everything and yet not touch anything. However, the atheist's position is even more extreme than that, for the atheist says in essence, "God is morally bound to go to such extremes to fix the problem of moral evil that he removes at least a good part of our autonomy. At the same time, it would be immoral of God to go to lesser extremes because to do so would infringe on our autonomy." You cannot demand A-level and B-level intervention and then cry "Unfair!" at mere C-level intervention that leaves autonomy basically intact.

Our Thesis

Thus we arrive at a very broad outline of what is to come. From the atheists' writings, we will discover two examples of what George Orwell called *doublethink*. As we shall see, the atheist holds two contradictory beliefs in his mind simultaneously, and moreover, he does it twice. These two fundamental inconsistencies will invalidate two central atheistic arguments. The first inconsistency overturns the atheist's argument appealing to the problem of moral evil. In the argument concerning moral evil, atheists claim that an all-loving, all-powerful, all-knowing God cannot exist alongside moral evil. In other words, because God does not intervene to fix the problem of moral evil, he is immoral, and thus, as an essentially moral being, nonexistent. Yet, as we will see, many atheists will contradict this argument against moral evil by going on to label as immoral the very interventions God would naturally use to fix the problem of moral evil. Why are these divine interventions immoral? The reason divine intervention becomes a problem for these atheists stems from the value they place on human autonomy. Divine intervention suppresses self-rule.

In their first inconsistency, the atheists' appeal to the problem of divine intervention seems to defeat their argument appealing to moral evil. Their second inconsistency then works to overturn their appeal to the problem of divine intervention. As we will see, the very interventions denounced at the divine, or theonomous, level are actually admitted to be necessary, even perhaps commendable, at the societal, or heteronomous, level. It turns out that these interventions are not immoral in themselves. If not immoral in themselves, why is God immoral to employ them, especially since they are the very interventions that will go to fix the problem of moral evil? Thus, those are the two inconsistencies to watch for. In order to resolve these two inconsistencies, the atheist will need to (1) drop either the argument appealing to the problem of moral evil or the arguments claiming that God's interventions to fix the problem of moral evil are immoral, and (2) stop labeling as immoral those interventions that the Christian God proposes while simultaneously claiming that their counterparts on the societal level are not immoral.

So our thesis is essentially an exposing of two fundamental inconsistencies that defeat two atheistic arguments. Thus the atheist basically crafts every argument in our book. One regiment marches under a banner that reads, "God Should Fix Everything"; another holds high the banner that says, "God Shouldn't Touch Anything." All the while, the opposite sides of each banner state the reverse: "Immoral for God, Moral for Humanity." Our aim is not a head-on rebuttal of any particular argument. Rather, our aim is to turn atheistic argument against atheistic argument until the inconsistency is recognized and one side of the argument is dropped. Inevitably, therefore, this book will be filled with quotations from atheists. In order to develop our charge of inconsistency, initially we will not have to argue, only to faithfully represent what the atheist is arguing.

1

The Problem of Moral Evil

It appears that even the Holocaust did not lead most Jews to doubt the existence of an omnipotent and benevolent God. If having half of your people systematically delivered to the furnace does not count as evidence against the notion that an all-powerful God is looking out for your interests, it seems reasonable to assume that nothing could.

—Sam Harris, *The End of Faith*[1]

Recall Richard Swinburne's claim: "The main argument against the existence of God has always been the 'argument from evil'—that is, from pain and malevolence."[2] Yet is the argument still the ace up the sleeve, the "gotcha," the knock-down punch today? More pointedly for this book, is the argument still made from pain *and* malevolence (i.e., natural evil *and* moral evil)? Or have the theodicies chipped away at the problem to where the "moral evil" horn has fallen off? To answer, note a television panel discussion as recalled by Richard Dawkins: "Swinburne at one point attempted to justify the Holocaust on the grounds that it gave the Jews a wonderful opportunity to be courageous and noble. Peter Atkins splendidly growled, 'May you rot in hell.'"[3] That debate apparently remains unsettled.

On the other hand, one could be pardoned for speculating that the argument from *moral* evil had lost its potency and dropped out of fashion. How else might we explain the emergence of formulations of the problem that seem to be crafted explicitly to sidestep traditional theistic responses to the problem of specifically moral evil? For example, a theist might respond that when the capacity for moral evil is taken away, so is the capacity for moral good. So the atheist might counter with an example of suffering that could not possibly produce moral good. Take, for instance, the celebrated statement of the problem by atheist William L. Rowe: "Suppose in some distant forest lightning strikes a dead tree, resulting in a forest fire. In the fire a fawn is trapped, horribly burned, and lies in terrible agony for several days before death relieves its suffering. So far as we can see, the fawn's intense suffering is pointless."[4] Aside from the obvious pity involved in the statement, one could almost detect a smirk: "Try your theodicy out on this one." In order to preclude traditional responses, the argument appropriates natural evil, not moral evil.

However, if one takes the time to read the works of recent and current leading advocates of atheism, as well as their heroes from the past, it becomes obvious that the problem of *moral* evil, not merely *natural* evil, remains a useful argument against the existence of a God who is both omnipotent and perfectly good. The aim of this chapter is to demonstrate the prominence of the problem of moral evil in today's rationale for atheism. The problem of moral evil is alleged to be God's fault in the first place, God's problem to fix in the meantime, and God's loss as exbelievers bear no blame for their exodus in light of the problem of moral evil. In each of these three sections, we will first consult the past heroes of today's atheists before considering the writings of recent and current atheists themselves.

God's Fault

If God were so good, why would his grandest creation turn out so bad? In the atheist's mind, even the most intelligently crafted redemptive plans can never hope to answer this single question. God can never redeem us enough to redeem himself from the initial fault of creating sinners. As the influential atheist Bertrand Russell framed it, "If I were going to beget a child knowing that the child was going to be a homicidal maniac, I should be responsible for his crimes. If God knew in advance the sins of which man would be guilty, he was clearly responsible for all the consequences of those sins when he decided to create man."[5] Elsewhere, Russell mused, "If [God is omnipotent], nothing contrary to his will can occur; therefore when the sinner disobeys his commands, he must have intended this to happen."[6] Carl Sagan put it bluntly: "Why is there such a long list of things that God tells people to do? Why didn't God do it right in the first place?"[7]

As eager as today's atheists are to denounce divine actions as not merely unnecessary or unhistorical but positively evil, it is no wonder that this argument is useful today. Not only are his demands, judgments, and redemptive plans evil but, as Creator, he himself created evil. According to Dan Barker, copresident of the Freedom from Religion Foundation,

> The Christian God cannot be both omniscient and omnibenevolent. If God were omniscient, then he knew when he created Adam that Adam would sin. He *knew* human beings would suffer. Regardless of whether the existence of evil can be theologically explicated, an all-knowing Creator deliberately placed humans in its path. This is at least criminal negligence, if not malice. Those who invoke "free will" forget that we all act according to a human nature that was

supposedly created by God himself. . . . At the moment of creation, an omniscient deity would have been picturing the suffering and damnation of most of his creation. This is mean-spirited. God should have had an abortion rather than bring a child into such misery.[8]

Again he writes, "If God knows in advance that there will be evil as a direct or indirect result of his actions, then he is not all-good. He is at least partly responsible for the harm."[9] Atheist Richard Carrier argues that God should have prepared us better for the potential of evil and, having failed to, is responsible for that evil:

> Likewise, as a loving parent, I would think it a horrible failure on my part if I didn't educate my children well, and supervise them kindly, teaching them how to live safe and well, and warning them of unknown or unexpected dangers. . . . It would be felony criminal neglect. Yet that is God: An absentee mom—who lets kids get kidnapped and murdered or run over by cars, who does nothing to teach them what they need to know, who never sits down like a loving parent to have an honest chat with them, and who would let them starve if someone else didn't intervene. As this is unconscionable, almost any idea of a god that fits the actual evidence of the world is unconscionable.[10]

Of course, in asking God to adopt such measures, the atheist volunteers to relinquish a measure of freedom. Yet atheist George Smith proposes a setup that retains freedom but restricts consequences. God's failure to shield the innocent is analogous to an unjust judicial system:

> Some men commit blatant injustices, but others do not. Some men murder, rob, and cheat, but others do not. Some men choose a policy of wanton destructiveness, but others do not. And we must remember that crimes are committed by men against other men, innocent victims, who cannot be held responsible. The minimum requirement for a civilized society is a legal system whereby the individual liberties of men are protected from the aggressive activities of

other men. We regard the recognition and protection of individual rights as a moral necessity, and we condemn governments that fail to provide a fair system of justice. How, then, are we to evaluate a God who permits widespread instances of injustice when it is easily within his power to prevent them?[11]

Abortion, better education, protection for the innocent—atheists can envision at least these three alternatives to God's plan. Since God failed to plan better, the problem of moral evil is ultimately his fault.

God's Problem

We might forgive a man for carelessly flicking a cigarette that ignited his barn, but we cannot forgive him for folding his arms as neighbors scramble to extinguish the fire. According to the atheist, it may be immoral for God to set evil in motion, but it is unconscionable for him to smirk from afar, watching us try pathetically to fix it. It is we who are chained to the problem; it is we who are forced to fix it. The religious have no extra, supernatural help; they merely have an extra chain that jerks their heads heavenward to pray their gratitude for something they themselves accomplished. It was this divine inertness that inspired Mark Twain to write,

> We hear much about His patience and forbearance and long-suffering; we hear nothing about our own, which much exceeds it. We hear much about His mercy and kindness and goodness. . . . There being no instances of it. . . .
> . . . The pulpit assures us that wherever we see suffering and sorrow, which we can relieve and do not do it, we sin, heavily. *There was never yet a case of suffering or sorrow which God could not relieve.* Does He sin, then?[12]

According to the heroes of today's atheists, a major share of this unforgivably unrelieved suffering is human evil. Russell asks,

"Do you think that, if you were granted omnipotence and omniscience and millions of years in which to perfect your world, you could produce nothing better than the Ku Klux Klan or the Fascists?"[13] Which atheist has not memorized the passage in which David Hume's Philo quotes the ancient atomist Epicurus: "Is he willing to prevent evil, but not able? Then he is impotent. Is he able, but not willing? Then he is malevolent. Is he both able and willing? Whence then is evil?"[14] It is worth noting Philo's preceding statement where, clearly, not just natural evil is in mind: "Man is the greatest enemy of man. Oppression, injustice, contempt, contumely, violence, sedition, war, calumny, treachery, fraud; by these they mutually torment each other."[15] Russell, too, lists "human sacrifices, persecutions of heretics, witch-hunts, pogroms leading up to wholesale extermination by poison gases," and starkly concludes, "If [the world in which we live] is the outcome of deliberate purpose, the purpose must have been that of a fiend."[16] God's nonintervention into the problem of moral evil translates into non-goodness, and on into nonexistence.

Rather than dropping the charges, today's atheists have only found more to add. Human evil is God's fault, and the more evil, the more of a mess awaits his cleanup. After all, there are many modern messes to pick from, as atheist Andrea M. Weisberger reminds us:

> Where was the intelligent designer of the universe when 1.5 million children were turned into smoke by zealous Nazis? Where was the all powerful, all knowing, wholly good being whose very essence is radically opposed to evil, while millions of children were starved to death by Stalin, had their limbs chopped off with machetes in Rwanda, were turned into amputees by the diamond trade in Sierra Leone, and worked to death, even now, by the child slave trade that, by conservative estimates, enslaves 250 million children worldwide? Without divine justice, all of this suffering is gratuitous. How, then, can a wholly good, all-powerful God be believed to exist?[17]

Recalling the Oklahoma City bombing, which injured 850 people, killed 168 (19 of which were children), and orphaned 30 children,[18] atheist Ian McEwan remarked, "The believers should know in their hearts by now that, even if they are right and there actually is a benign and watchful personal God, he is, as all the daily tragedies, all the dead children attest, a reluctant intervener. The rest of us, in the absence of any evidence to the contrary, know that it is highly improbable that there is anyone up there at all."[19]

In addition to finding new examples of evil, today's atheists have devised novel formulations of the problem of evil, in which moral evil plays a part. It is important to realize that often even statements of the problem of evil that appear to have excluded moral evil completely cannot prevent moral evil from becoming intertwined in the argument. For example, a nation's poverty and starvation can sometimes be directly linked to greedy dictators hoarding the nation's wealth, even the foreign aid meant for their destitute people. Similarly, when atheist John Loftus claims in his "Darwinian Problem of Evil" that animal suffering is irreconcilable with the goodness of God, he inevitably brings in the problem of moral evil: "Human beings rule over the animal kingdom with an iron fist. Almost every kind of living creature is eaten as food by at least some of us on the planet."[20] Also note Loftus's argument against God based on his "failure to communicate." According to Loftus, God should have been able to communicate his Word in such a clear way as to prevent the many diverse and dangerous interpretations of the Bible throughout history. Here again we find the problem of moral evil at work: "God created us with the very propensities we have for misunderstanding and violence, otherwise we wouldn't be in this mess in the first place."[21]

From their writings, we can piece together three reasons today's atheists believe God should be intervening in the problem of moral evil: God's inaction goes against the precedent we find in the Bible, the inclination we find in ourselves, and the love we expect from God. According to the first reason, assuming God has not developed arthritis or something, should he not intervene as in the glorious days of old? He could back then, right? Bart Ehrman's path to becoming a skeptical New Testament critic was, by his admission, from Christian fundamentalism to agnosticism via the problem of evil. He retraces the thoughts leading to his deconversion: "If God intervened to deliver the armies of Israel from its enemies, why doesn't he intervene now when the armies of sadistic tyrants savagely attack and destroy entire villages, towns, and even countries?"[22]

The second reason God should intervene is that nonintervention goes against the inclination we find in ourselves. God should because we would. We are neither as good nor as powerful as God, yet even we would do at least whatever we could to intervene. As one whose goodness and ability are infinite, he thus has no conceivable excuse for not intervening. According to Carrier,

> It's a simple fact of direct observation that if *I* had the means and the power, and could not be harmed for my efforts, I would immediately alleviate all needless suffering in the universe. . . . And whenever men and women seemed near to violence, I would intervene and kindly endeavor to help them peacefully resolve their differences. That's what any loving person would do. Yet I cannot be more loving, more benevolent than the Christian God. Therefore, the fact that the Christian God does none of these things—in fact, nothing of any sort whatsoever—is proof positive that there is no Christian God.[23]

Not only would intervention be the loving action to take, but also, according to Weisberger, such action is morally obligatory:

> There is an abundance of evil in our world. If we can prevent it, then we are morally obligated to do so. How much more obligated a per-fectly powerful and perfectly good God must be to do the same? The theist, who maintains that such a God exists, must explain why this abundance of evil persists and why the number of rapes, murders,

child torturers, serial killers, bombings, animal cruelties, and the like proliferate at a rate that threatens to exhaust and suffocate us.[24]

The third reason God should intervene is that nonintervention directly contradicts the love attributed to the Christian God. The Bible may associate nonintervention with noble-sounding goals like patience or character building, but atheists perceive such non-intervention as nothing short of cruel. A candid Steven Weinberg remarked, "Remembrance of the Holocaust leaves me unsympathetic to attempts to justify the ways of God to man. If there is a God that has special plans for humans, then he has taken very great pains to hide his concern for us."[25] To Carrier, it is as straightforward as "Socrates is mortal":

> Think about it. A man approaches a school with a loaded assault rifle, intent on mass slaughter. A loving person speaks to him, attempts to help him resolve his problems or to persuade him to stop, and failing that, punches him right in the kisser, and takes away his gun. And a loving person with godlike powers could simply turn his bullets into popcorn as they left the gun, or heal with a touch whatever insanity or madness (or by teaching him cure whatever ignorance) led the man to contemplate the crime. But God does nothing. Therefore, a loving God does not exist.[26]

For atheist Sam Harris, such inaction is unthinkable, or at least it should be:

> Somewhere in the world a man has abducted a little girl. Soon he will rape, torture, and kill her. . . . Such is the confidence we can draw from the statistical laws that govern the lives of six billion human beings. The same statistics also suggest that this girl's parents believe—as you believe—that an all-powerful and all-loving God is watching over them and their family. Are they right to believe this? Is it *good* that they believe this?
> No.
> The entirety of atheism is contained in this response.[27]

Hence, "An atheist is a person who believes that the murder of a single little girl—even once in a million years—casts doubt upon the idea of a benevolent God."[28] For Harris, this is the final nail in God's coffin. The discussion is over: "The problem of vindicating an omnipotent and omniscient God in the face of evil . . . is insurmountable."[29]

God's Loss

Since the problem of moral evil is God's fault in the first place and his problem to deal with, it is no surprise that the problem remains an admittedly decisive reason many turn away from him. Not only is the problem of moral evil an argument used by atheists, but also, in many cases, it is *the* decisive argument, the blow that breaks their hold on God in the first place. Former atheist Antony Flew recalls,

> One of those early reasons for my conversion to atheism was the problem of evil. . . .
>
> I was greatly influenced by these early travels abroad [particularly to Germany] during the years before World War II. I vividly recall the banners and signs outside small towns proclaiming, "Jews not wanted here." I remember signs outside the entrance to a public library proclaiming, "The regulations of this institution forbid the issuing of any books to Jewish borrowers." I observed a march of ten thousand brown-shirted storm troopers through a Bavarian summer night. Our family travels exposed me to squads of the Waffen-SS in their black uniforms with skull-and-crossbones caps. Such experiences sketched the background of my youthful life and for me, as for many others, presented an inescapable challenge to the existence of an all-powerful God of love. The degree to which they influenced my thinking I cannot measure.[30]

According to Ehrman, "The problem of suffering has haunted me for a very long time. It was what made me begin to think about religion when I was young, and it was what led me to question my faith when I was older. Ultimately, it was the reason I lost my faith."[31] For Carrier, God's inertness in the face of evil is one of four reasons he gives for why he became an atheist.[32] Atheist comedian George Carlin even wove the problem into his comedy routine:

> When it comes to believing in God, I really tried. I really, really tried. I tried to believe that there is a God, who created each of us in His own image and likeness, loves us very much, and keeps a close eye on things. I really tried to believe that, but I gotta tell you, the longer you live, the more you look around, the more you realize . . . something is wrong here. War, disease, death, destruction, hunger, filth, poverty, torture, crime, corruption, and the Ice Capades. Something is definitely wrong. This is not good work. If this is the best God can do, I am not impressed. Results like these do not belong on the resume of a Supreme Being. This is the kind of [stuff] you'd expect from an office temp with a bad attitude.[33]

And who can forget the former pulpit partner of Billy Graham, Charles Templeton, whose book *Farewell to God* argued that one's faith in God cannot survive exposure to rationality? In response to the question, "Was there one thing in particular that caused you to lose your faith in God?" he narrowed his eyes and replied,

> It was a photograph in *Life* magazine. . . . It was a picture of a black woman in Northern Africa. They were experiencing a devastating drought. And she was holding her dead baby in her arms and looking up to heaven with the most forlorn expression. I looked at it and I thought, "Is it possible to believe that there is a loving Creator when all this woman needed was *rain*?"[34]

Swastikas, torture, despots hoarding food during drought—much more than a back-breaking straw, the problem of moral evil is a back-breaking camel. For these atheists, it was soul freeing to give up trying to balance the goodness of God with the weight of evil. It is off their backs, and in their estimation, it is not their loss.

Our Greatest Enemy?

The point has been made that, in their arguments, today's atheists employ the problem of moral evil. For our purposes, that is what is necessary to proceed to the next chapter. However, the potency of the problem of moral evil is another issue. Perhaps if it can be shown that the problem of moral evil is indeed a *major* problem to atheists—and if the central contentions of this book prove sound—then our contentions will have dealt a blow to a major atheistic argument. It has already been shown that the problem of evil has persuaded many toward atheism and that *moral* evil has played a significant role in those arguments. How significant, though? Is natural evil the real culprit, with moral evil being an impish sidekick? It seems the answer is no; in fact it may be closer to the other way around. In his book on evil, *Unspeakable*, sociologist Os Guinness titled his chapter on human evil "Our Greatest Enemy."[35] Though many atheists will scorn such indictments and persist in trumpeting the goodness of humanity, it seems that the atheist with eyes open would agree.

At the very least, human beings, in contrast to animals, seem to be more culpable for moral wrongdoing. As Barker puts it, "If you look at nature, you discover that there is very little crime in the plant kingdom. (Ignoring dandelions.) Is it a felony when an eagle kills a field mouse? Immorality, crime, malice and cruelty belong to the 'higher' forms of life."[36] Thomas Hobbes spoke more forcefully: "Man is the most cunning, the strongest, and most dangerous animal."[37] Stronger still was Voltaire, in a letter following the Lisbon earthquake that left sixty thousand dead: "I pity the Portuguese, like you, but men do still more harm to each other on their little molehill than nature does to them. Our wars massacre more men than are swallowed up by earthquakes."[38] Voltaire was prophetic; according to Weisberger,

> The type of suffering that results from the actions of moral agents perhaps dwarfs the vast amount of suffering caused by natural

disasters. An estimated 20–30 million were starved to death in Stalin's purges, approximately 9 million were killed by Hitler's Third Reich, and at least 3 million were murdered by Pol Pot's Khmer Rouge. In the United States alone it is estimated that 60 million animals a year are sacrificed on the altar of fast food. Millions of others are tortured to provide profits for pharmaceutical mega-corporations. All of this is planned and executed by "moral" agents.[39]

Most natural disasters and even plagues seem to grant respites. Yet historian Will Durant estimates that throughout all history there might have been only twenty-nine years in which there were no wars being fought anywhere.[40] According to Hume's Philo, "Moral evil, in the opinion of many, is much more predominant above moral good than natural evil above natural good."[41] It seems Hume's Philo was correct in concluding, "Man is the greatest enemy of man."[42] But of course the atheist goes one step more and concludes that thus man's Creator must be a greater enemy still.

2

The Value of Human Autonomy

I have repeatedly said that in my opinion the idea of a personal God is a childlike one. You may call me an agnostic, but I do not share the crusading spirit of the professional atheist whose fervor is mostly due to a painful act of liberation from the fetters of religious indoctrination received in youth.

—Albert Einstein, personal letter[1]

Since in our past our parents died on average younger than they do today . . . we created god(s) to fill that gap. God belief is a kind of delayed development. . . . Getting rid of the "father-figure agency" is a part of maturing. It is a sign of mental health, and the only way to truly grow up.

—Dan Barker, *Godless*[2]

The atheist thinks God ought to have prevented initially or ought to prevent each day the problem of moral evil. Of course, the question then becomes how to accomplish this. Recall that the possible interventions into the problem can be categorized as intervention into all cases (A level), in the truly bad cases (B level), or merely on the conscience level for the willing (C level). Since the atheist is clearly asking God to do more to fix the problem of moral evil than God has already done, the atheist is asking for either A- or B-level interventions. Practically, this means either constraints on humanity's ability to commit certain acts or the thwarting of the acts once attempted. In other words, what the atheist is asking God for would mean a radically diminished human autonomy.

Yet, as this chapter will make clear, atheists are not at all shy about their affection for autonomy, the freedom to rule one's own self. As we will see in coming chapters, the atheist ends up rejecting as immoral the very interventions God would logically use to fix the problem of moral evil. But this is inconsistent: why reject these requested interventions? This chapter helps provide an explanation. The point of this chapter is to allow the atheists to prove their devotion to autonomy. As we will see in coming chapters, when interventions approach, autonomy feels threatened, and this devotion comes to autonomy's defense. Though this devotion to autonomy does not excuse the inconsistencies we will see, it helps explain them.

Growing Up

Of course, it must be admitted from the outset that humanity *once* needed God. In fact, says the atheist, that is precisely how he showed up in the first place; we dreamed him up and invited him in. According to atheist Ludwig Feuerbach, what we idolized in ourselves became embodied and enthroned as actual idols:

> The object of any subject is nothing else than the subject's own nature taken objectively. Such as are a man's thoughts and dispositions,

such is his God; so much worth as a man has, so much and no more has his God. Consciousness of God is self-consciousness, knowledge of God is self-knowledge. By his God thou knowest the man, and by the man his God; the two are identical.[3]

After Feuerbach, atheist Sigmund Freud specified which strata of man became divinized—the father:

> As we already know, the terrifying impression of helplessness in childhood aroused the need for protection—for protection through love—which was provided by the father; and the recognition that this helplessness lasts throughout life made it necessary to cling to the existence of a father, but this time a more powerful one. Thus the benevolent rule of a Divine Providence allays our fear of the dangers of life; the establishment of a moral world-order ensures the fulfillment of the demands of justice.[4]

"The God idea," says atheist and anarchist Emma Goldman, expressed "a sort of spiritualistic stimulus to satisfy the fads and fancies of every shade of human weakness."[5]

Inevitably, however, the time comes to leave the nest. Freud hints that it is past time:

> [Religion] has ruled human society for many thousands of years and has had time to show what it can achieve. If it had succeeded in making the majority of mankind happy, in comforting them, in reconciling them to life and in making them into vehicles of civilization, no one would dream of attempting to alter the existing conditions. But what do we see instead? We see that an appallingly large number of people are dissatisfied with civilization and unhappy in it, and feel it as a yoke which must be shaken off.[6]

The *Humanist Manifesto 2000* agrees: "We think it time for humanity to embrace its own adulthood—to leave behind magical thinking and mythmaking that are substitutes for tested knowledge of nature."[7] After all, says Feuerbach, "Religion is the childlike condition of humanity."[8] And when I became a man, I put childish things behind me. For example, says atheist Michel Onfray, "We need no posthumous paradise, no salvation or redemption of the soul, no all-knowing, all-seeing God."[9] Not only do we not need God, but we *need* to no longer need him. As Goldman puts it, the concept of God "has dominated humanity and will continue to do so until man will raise his head to the sunlit day, unafraid and with an awakened will to himself. . . . How far man will be able to find his relation to his fellows will depend entirely upon how much he can outgrow his dependence upon God."[10]

Such a coming-of-age should be predictable in any healthy society. As Feuerbach foretold, "What yesterday was still religion is no longer such today; and what today is atheism, tomorrow will be religion."[11] Auguste Comte likewise predicted the coming maturity in his three stages of humanity: theological childhood, metaphysical youth, and scientific, "positive" adulthood.[12] Moreover, there have been periods in which such predictions seem to have come true. For example, regarding the French Revolution, we are told of the march on the Notre Dame Cathedral, where "they enthroned a dancer of doubtful morals as 'the goddess of Reason.'"[13] It seems here we grew up ethically, to a "dancer of doubtful morals"; metaphysically, to a "goddess"; and epistemologically, to "Reason." In fact, was not the period affectionately known as the Enlightenment precisely a mass exodus from childhood to the university? After this triumph of reason, nature, and progress, even though the masses still flocked to and frenzied around the grave of a Jansenist priest said to have performed healings, a new authority had arisen that could, for example, bar the cemetery off with a sign that said, "By order of the king, God is forbidden to make miracles in this place."[14] At least some of humanity was growing up. Yet even after such predictions and periods of progress, adulthood still eludes us and enlightenment still waits, according to Onfray:

We can and we must subscribe to the Enlightenment which remains as viable as ever. It aims to lift man out infantile condition and set his feet on the path to adul to remind him of his own responsibility for his infantile state; to inspire him with the courage to use his intelligence; to give himself and others the capacity to attain self-mastery; to make public and communal use of his reason in every field, with no exception; and not to accept as revealed truth what emanates from public authority.[15]

Of course, as in Plato's cave, there are those who can handle the brightness and those who cannot. There will always be the antediluvian grouches who reminisce about the "good ol' Dark Ages" and scowl at progress. There will always be gawking masses herding to the weeping statue. Freud laments, "Civilization has little to fear from educated people and brain-workers. . . . But it is another matter with the great mass of the uneducated and oppressed."[16] Their belief in the Father "is so obviously infantile, so far from reality, that it is painful to anyone with convictions friendly toward humanity to think that the great majority of mortals will never be able to rise above this view of life."[17] But perhaps more education can tip the scale toward atheism. According to atheist Percy Bysshe Shelley, "It is among men of genius and science that Atheism alone is found, but among these alone is cherished an hostility to those errors, with which the illiterate and vulgar are infected."[18] Atheist Daniel Dennett proposes a new name for these lights in society: "A bright is a person with a naturalist as opposed to a supernaturalist world view. We brights don't believe in ghosts or elves or the Easter Bunny—or God."[19] The future belongs to the kind of person atheist Friedrich Nietzsche envisioned in his introduction to *The Antichrist*:

> This book belongs to the most rare of men. Perhaps not one of them is yet alive. . . .

. . . He must have an inclination, born of strength, for questions
that no one has the courage for; the courage for the forbidden;
predestination for the labyrinth. . . .
. . . The rest are merely humanity.[20]

A convert from Christianity to atheism and back again, A. N.
Wilson describes what it was like to finally be counted among the
initiates:

> For the first time in my 38 years I was at one with my own genera-
> tion. I had become like one of the Billy Grahamites, only in reverse.
> If I bumped into Richard Dawkins (an old colleague from Oxford
> days) or had dinner in Washington with Christopher Hitchens (as
> I did either on that trip to interview Billy Graham or another), I
> did not have to feel out on a limb. Hitchens was excited to greet a
> new convert to his non-creed and put me through a catechism be-
> fore uncorking some stupendous claret. "So—absolutely no God?"
> "Nope," I was able to say with Moonie-zeal.[21]

Former atheist Paul Vitz admits that a "major reason for my becoming an atheist was that I desired to be accepted by the powerful
and influential scientists in the field of psychology."[22] Former atheist Peter Hitchens recounts his fascination: "I had spotted the dry,
disillusioned, and apparently disinterested atheism of so many
intellectuals, artists, and leaders of our age. I liked their crooked
smiles, their knowing worldliness, and their air of finding human
credulity amusing."[23]

And then, of course, with God no longer towering over humanity,
who better to commence building to the heavens than those who
cleared the way in the first place? After any death, the question of
"who gets what" inevitably turns up. God's murder is no exception, as Nietzsche's madman explains: "Is not the greatness of this
deed too great for us? Must not we ourselves become gods simply
to seem worthy of it? There has never been a greater deed; and
whoever will be born after us—for the sake of this deed he will be

part of a higher history than all history hitherto."[24] The *Humanist Manifesto II* says the same only with less theatrics: "While there is much that we do not know, humans are responsible for what we are or will become. No deity will save us; we must save ourselves."[25]

Casting Off

Now, while it is true that some atheists reminisce about meager contributions religion might have made in our early development, the tone hardens from patronizing to despising when religion continues trying to parent. Anticipating attempts at subjugation, the atheist has crafted an entire worldview centered on autonomy, all tethers cut and cast off. We find that the central questions comprising one's worldview are the following:

Origin: Where did we come from?

Identity: Who are we?

Meaning: Why are we here?

Morality: How shall we live?

Destiny: Where are we going?[26]

In each of these five most consequential areas of life, the atheist insists on freedom.

First, obviously, the atheist demands freedom of origin. As Peter Atkins frames it, scientific man simply has no need for a creating, designing, purposing, intervening, loving, or umpiring God. He contends,

> The assertion that God did anything is simplistic rather than simple, and it is lazy. It is simplistic because an entity as functionally unbounded as a God must be of extraordinary complexity. It is lazy because it avoids becoming involved in untangling the web of events that have led to us. Any argument that simply asserts that "God did it" is a sign of a lazy mind, a mind that is content to wallow in

assertion rather than embark upon climbing the intellectual Everest of comprehension.[27]

Thus, atheists busy themselves devising theories postulating such phenomena as multiple universes, directed panspermia, Darwinian evolution, and punctuated equilibrium at least in part to explain our origin without the "lazy" resort to God.

Second, the atheist demands freedom of identity. Atheism is the identity's emancipation, says Goldman: "Atheism in its negation of gods is at the same time the strongest affirmation of man, and through man, the eternal yea to life, purpose, and beauty."[28] This is because religion is man's demotion, according to atheist Karl Marx: "The criticism of religion ends with the teaching that *man is the highest essence for man*, hence with the *categoric imperative to overthrow all relations* in which man is a debased, enslaved, abandoned, despicable essence."[29] To relinquish one's identity under God can be a tough imperative to carry out, especially to the once devout. Former evangelist Dan Barker knows, but he nurses no regrets. He describes his realization that he was "completely and utterly alone" as

> simultaneously a frightening and liberating experience. Maybe first-time skydivers or space walkers have a similar sensation. I just knew that everything had come to rest, that the struggle was over, that I had truly shed the cocoon and I was, for the first time in my life, that "new creature" of which the Bible so ignorantly speaks. I had at last graduated from the childish need to look outside myself to decide who I was as a person.[30]

Third, the atheist demands freedom of meaning. It is true, he admits, that having God in one's life can infuse a sort of meaning, but it is not the kind the atheist desires. According to Richard Dawkins, such borrowed meaning is all part of the babyish solipsism that needs to be outgrown:

There is something infantile in the presumption that somebody else (parents in the case of children, God in the case of adults) has a responsibility to give your life meaning and point. It is all of a piece with the infantilism of those who, the moment they twist their ankle, look around for someone to sue. Somebody else must be responsible for my well-being, and somebody else must be to blame if I am hurt.[31]

After all, says Barker, meaning is so much more meaningful when we create it ourselves: "There is purpose *in* life. If there were a purpose *of* life, then that would cheapen life. It would make us tools or slaves of someone else's purpose. . . . Our value would not be in ourselves. It would exist in our submission to the will of the toolmaker. That is slavery to a master, or infant dependency on a father figure."[32]

Fourth, the atheist demands freedom of morality. Atheist Christopher Hitchens asks,

Who wishes that there was a permanent, unalterable celestial despotism that subjected us to continual surveillance and could convict us of thought-crime, and who regarded us as its private property even after we died? How happy we ought to be, at the reflection that there exists not a shred of respectable evidence to support such a horrible hypothesis. And how grateful we should be to those of our predecessors who repudiated this utter negation of human freedom.[33]

The only surveillance we need comes from within, as atheist Salman Rushdie explains:

As for morality, the second great question—how to live? what is right action, and what wrong?—it comes down to your willingness to think for yourself. Only you can decide if you want to be handed down the law by priests and accept that good and evil are somehow external to ourselves. To my mind religion, even at its most sophisticated, essentially infantilizes our ethical selves by setting infallible moral Arbiters and irredeemably immoral Tempt-ers above us: the eternal parents, good and bad, light and dark, of the supernatural realm.[34]

We might need morality from without if we were corrupt within, but we are not, says Barker: "The New Testament Jesus reportedly said, 'They that are whole have no need of a physician, but they that are sick' (Matt. 9:12). We atheists consider ourselves whole, thank you. We are not sick. We don't need the doctor."[35]

Fifth, atheists demand freedom of destiny. According to the *Humanist Manifesto 2000*, "As humanists we urge today, as in the past, that humans not look beyond themselves for salvation. We alone are responsible for our own destiny, and the best we can do is muster our intelligence, courage, and compassion to realize our highest aspirations."[36] Goldman agrees: "In proportion as man learns to realize himself and mold his own destiny, theism becomes superflu-ous. How far man will be able to find his relation to his fellows will depend entirely upon how much he can outgrow his dependence upon God."[37] How does this realization take place? "Man must break his fetters which have chained him to the gates of heaven and hell, so that he can begin to fashion out of his reawakened and illumined consciousness a new world upon earth."[38] Bertrand Russell offers utopian prescriptions: "It is possible that mankind is on the threshold of a golden age; but, if so, it will be necessary to slay the dragon that guards the door, and this dragon is religion."[39]

Marching On

Like colonists on the original July 4, all "Atheistendom" is giddy with the prospect of freedom. Perhaps Lucretius's ancient prophecy will be fulfilled in our lifetime:

> Then how in turn underfoot Religion is hurled down and trampled,
> Then how that victory lifts mankind to high level of heaven.[40]

Dawkins thinks victory is within grasp, thanks to the march of science:

> Could we, by training and practice, emancipate ourselves from Middle World [the realm between the microscopic and the galactic], tear off our black burka, and achieve some sort of intuitive—as well as just mathematical—understanding of the very small, the very large, and the very fast? I genuinely don't know the answer, but I am thrilled to be alive at a time when humanity is pushing against the limits of understanding. Even better, we may eventually discover that there are no limits.[41]

Dawkins speaks of the glorious march of a liberator, for "when given the right encouragement to think for themselves about all the information now available" people "very often turn out *not* to believe in God and to lead fulfilled and satisfied—indeed, *liberated*—lives."[42] After all, liberation from God means uninhibited autonomy. For some reason, however, though Dawkins understands and praises the liberation of atheists from God, he cannot understand why the ancient Israelites enjoyed the same prospect:

> But the apparently irresistible temptation to whore with foreign gods is something we moderns find harder to empathize with. To my naïve eyes, "Thou shalt have no other gods but me" would seem an easy enough commandment to keep. . . . Yet throughout the Old Testament, with the same predictable regularity as in bedroom farce, God had only to turn his back for a moment and the Children of Israel would be off and at it with Baal, or some trollop of a graven image.[43]

As Dawkins points out, excitement at the prospect of liberation from God is nothing new.

There has of yet been no contradiction. The atheist requests that God do something to fix the problem of moral evil. Then comes the breakup: God won't comply, so I won't stick around.

The language changes from "if he existed" to "since he doesn't exist." And so, reasons the atheist, since he doesn't exist, let's enjoy our autonomy. Let's patronize our skyward devotion for the elementary silliness that it is! Let's celebrate our fortunate origins and escalating identities. Let's adopt unfettered moralities for our customized meanings. Let's dream up brave new destinies. What thrilling prospects! As of yet, we find no inconsistency, only an impulse. Autonomy is a cherished value, such that atheists transform into preachy-Nietzsche revivalists for its gospel. As we will see in the chapters to come, atheists pursue it long and hard, even unto contradiction.

3

Submission and Favor

[Religious faith] manages to combine the maximum of servility with the maximum of solipsism.

—Christopher Hitchens, *God Is Not Great*[1]

In chapter 1, we discovered that many atheists appeal to the problem of moral evil to disprove God's existence. In chapter 2, we discovered that though the atheist decries the moral evil made possible by human autonomy, the atheist remains committed to valuing human autonomy. Thus we will see in the next five chapters how the atheist responds when divine interventions into the problem of moral evil are actually proposed. Each of these five chapters is dedicated to a pair of interventions within God's plan proposed to fix the problem of moral evil. What will the atheist say when, in the cause of virtue, he is asked to voluntarily surrender a measure of his autonomy? The first pair of interventions we explore is submission and favor. Both are paired nicely by Ludwig Feuerbach:

Man—this is the mystery of religion—projects his being into objectivity, and then again makes himself an object to this projected image of himself thus converted into a subject. . . . Thus the religious man virtually retracts the nothingness of human activity, by making his dispositions and actions an object to God, by making man the end of God—for that which is an object to the mind is an end in action; by making the divine activity a means of human salvation. God acts, that man may be good and happy. Thus man, while he is apparently humiliated to the lowest degree, is in truth exalted to the highest.[2]

What Submission Says about God

To the atheist, any god who asks for submission is a tyrant. According to Dan Barker, the first three problems with using the Bible as a guide for morality are the following:

1. The Bible argues from authority, not from reason, claiming that "might makes right."
2. The Bible nowhere states that every human being possesses an inherent right to be treated with respect and fairness—humans don't matter as much as God does.
3. The biblical role models, especially Yahweh, Elohim, and Jesus, are very poor moral examples, often ignoring their own good teachings (what few there are) and ruthlessly pursuing their own tyrannical teachings.[3]

In other words, God is all about God. All of life trembles in the shadow of his agenda, his power, his will, his teachings. Such a God is selfish, says Feuerbach:

In brief, man in relation to God denies his own knowledge, his own thoughts, that he may place them in God. Man gives up his personality; but in return, God, the Almighty, infinite, unlimited being is a person; he denies human dignity, the human *ego*; but in return

God is to him a selfish, egoistical being, who in all things seeks only himself, his own honour, his own ends; he represents God as simply seeking the satisfaction of his own selfishness, while yet he frowns on that of every other being; his God is the very luxury of egoism.[4]

The widely traveled journalist Christopher Hitchens cannot resist drawing a comparison:

> In the early months of this century, I made a visit to North Korea. Here, contained within a hermetic quadrilateral of territory enclosed either by sea or by near-impenetrable frontiers, is a land entirely given over to adulation. Every waking moment of the citizen—the subject—is consecrated to praise of the Supreme Being and his Father. Every schoolroom resounds with it, every film and opera and play is devoted to it, every radio and television transmission is given up to it. So are all books and magazines and newspaper articles, all sporting events and all workplaces. I used to wonder what it would be like to have to sing everlasting praises, and now I know.[5]

Bertrand Russell agrees with the parallel: "In the orthodox Christian conception, the good life is the virtuous life, and virtue consists in obedience to the will of God, and the will of God is revealed to each individual through the voice of conscience. This whole conception is that of men subject to an alien despotism."[6] "Barbarity, caprice," David Hume calls it. "These qualities, however nominally disguised, we may universally observe, form the ruling character of the deity in the popular religions. . . . The more tremendous the divinity is represented, the more tame and submissive do men become his ministers."[7] What makes such despotism so barbaric, however, is the scope of its demand. Hitchens labels this call to complete submission *totalitarianism* because it "separates 'ordinary' forms of despotism—those which merely exact obedience from their subjects—from the absolutist systems which demand that citizens become wholly subjects and surrender their private lives and personalities entirely to the state, or to the supreme leader."[8]

To willfully place oneself under such a regime is "to *wish* for your own subjection, and to delight in the subjection of others."[9]

It might be asked, however, What if such a God is actually worthy of entire submission? What if, once you got to know him, you actually wanted such a relationship? The atheist responds that he already knows enough about God to convince him that this will never happen. Sam Harris seems confident enough: "We know enough at this moment to say that the God of Abraham is not only unworthy of the immensity of creation; he is unworthy even of man."[10] According to Russell, "The nonhuman world is unworthy of our worship."[11] Nietzsche clarified,

> The thing that sets us apart is not that we are unable to find God, either in history, or in nature, or behind nature—but that we regard what has been honored as God, not as "divine," but as pitiable, as absurd, as injurious; not as a mere error, but as a crime against life. . . . We deny that God is God. . . . If any one were to show us this Christian God, we'd be still less inclined to believe in him.[12]

Note that the atheist is not suggesting that because God does not exist, it is irrational to submit to him. The contention is that the God presented in Christianity, whether or not he exists, is positively immoral to demand such submission. Just who does he think he is? And, for that matter, who does he think we are?

What Submission Says about Us

While the demand for submission enlarges God into a tyrant, it dwarfs man into a stuttering servant. Under God's thumb, we are squashed into perpetual infancy. Hitchens paints the unflattering portrait:

> The three great monotheisms teach people to think abjectly of themselves, as miserable and guilty sinners prostrate before an angry

and jealous god who, according to discrepant accounts, fashioned them either out of dust and clay or a clot of blood. The positions for prayer are usually emulations of the supplicant serf before an ill-tempered monarch. The message is one of continual submission, gratitude, and fear.[13]

According to Barker, enough time in such a posture cripples us:

> One of the most damaging ideas in the Bible is the concept of Lord and Master. The loftiest biblical principles are obedience, submission and faith, rather than reason, intelligence and human values. Worshippers become humble servants of a dictator, expected to kneel before this king, lord, master, god—giving adoring praise and taking orders.[14]

In fact, because all religious faith demands submission, then naturally all religion by definition stunts humanity. Feuerbach explains the process by which religion arises: "To enrich God, man must become poor; that God may be all, man must be nothing."[15] Nietzsche writes, "The man of faith, the 'believer' of any sort, is necessarily a dependent man—such a man cannot posit himself as a goal, nor can he find goals within himself. The 'believer' does not belong to himself; he can only be a means to an end."[16] As Russell puts it, "The whole conception of God is a conception derived from the ancient Oriental despotisms. It is a conception quite unworthy of free men. When you hear people in church debasing themselves and saying that they are miserable sinners, and all the rest of it, it seems contemptible and not worthy of self-respecting human beings."[17]

How then might a self-respecting human respond to such a God? Perhaps the most courteous response is a firm "No, thanks." Mature man has no need of that hypothesis. According to the *Humanist Manifesto II*, "Too often traditional faiths encourage dependence rather than independence, obedience rather than affirmation, fear rather than courage."[18] The *Humanist Manifesto I* prescribes, "In place of the old attitudes involved in worship and prayer the humanist finds his religious emotions expressed in a heightened sense of personal life and in a cooperative effort to promote social well-being."[19] The old-fashioned supplicant remains in the clutches of fear. In an ironic twist, Russell quips, "Fear is the main source of superstition and one of the main sources of cruelty. To conquer fear is the beginning of wisdom."[20] Fear of the Lord is too babyish. Besides, a good parent would not nurture belief in closet ghosts so that he or she could be called upon each night. Barker explains, "A true father expects the child to become a peer, with its own purpose, even if it disagrees with the parent. If I raise a child who is eternally dependent on me for meaning, then I am an inept parent."[21] Thus we graduate from the comfort of the parent's lap to the productivity of the laboratory. Says Russell, "Science can teach us, and I think our own hearts can teach us, no longer to look around for imaginary supports, no longer to invent allies in the sky, but rather to look to our own efforts here below to make this world a fit place to live in, instead of the sort of place that the churches in all these centuries have made it."[22] After all, if we do not grow up, we will remain one species under God instead of rising to become the supreme species ourselves. It is either he or we, as philosopher Walter Kaufmann explains:

> The basic choice is this: either man hypostatizes the object of his profoundest aspirations, projects his boldest hopes, and in the most extreme case strips himself of all that distinguishes him from the apes, and then the ape that remains grovels on his belly; or man seeks to leave the ape behind on the ground and tries to raise himself to a higher level of being. Whether he worships idols or strives to perfect himself, man is the God-intoxicated ape.[23]

But what of the believer's customary reply: Unless you submit to God, will you not succumb to reprobation? Richard Dawkins thinks not: "Do we really need policing—whether by God or by each other—in order to stop us from behaving in a selfish and criminal manner? I dearly want to believe that I do not need such surveillance—and nor, dear reader, do you."[24] Hitchens agrees: "Most important of all, perhaps, we infidels do not need any machinery of reinforcement."[25] Thus, "There is no need for us to gather every day, or every seven days, or on any high and auspicious day, to proclaim our rectitude or to grovel and wallow in our unworthiness. We atheists do not require any priests, or any hierarchy above them, to police our doctrine."[26]

Hence, if a good humanity does not need to bow and a truly good God would not need us to either, we will not bow. Such refusal is atheism, according to Emma Goldman: "Atheism . . . in its philosophic aspect refuses allegiance not merely to a definite concept of God, but it refuses all servitude to the God idea."[27] For Barker, it is either God or the individual: "Jesus said, 'Render therefore unto Caesar the things which are Caesar's; and unto God the things that are God's.' But what about the individual? What about democracy? . . . It is not moral to be told to submit to a Caesar or to a god."[28] Even gratitude is demeaning, as Daniel Dennett argues in his article "Thank Goodness." After making it through a nine-hour heart surgery, he chose to thank "goodness." Of course, "You can thank God—but the very idea of repaying God is ludicrous."[29] Similarly, after Barker's wife pulled through a near-fatal infant delivery, Barker boasted, much like a new mother in not having requested an epidural, "During this entire traumatic experience we never once thought of invoking a god for help. We never prayed, never even considered it."[30] Thus, to Hitchens, the response is obvious: get up off the floor.

> My old schoolfriend Michael Prest was the first person to make it plain to me that while the authorities could compel us to attend prayers, they could not force us to pray. I shall always remember his upright posture while others hypocritically knelt or inclined

themselves, and also the day that I decided to join him. All postures
of submission and surrender should be part of our prehistory.[31]

Favor: Vanity of the Species

Since the atheist is so violently opposed to being treated as a
slave, it seems he would appreciate adoption into a more esteemed
position. What would the atheist say if God were to exalt what
he humbled, to stoop to our level in order to elevate us closer
to his? Yet just as the atheist translates submission as tyranny,
divine favor is rejected as bribery, and the atheist will have none
of it. For one thing, such tactics only go to satiate mankind's
conceit. According to Russell, "Religion has, however, other appeals besides that of terror; it appeals especially to our human
self-esteem. If Christianity is true, mankind are not such pitiful
worms as they seem to be; they are of interest to the Creator of
the universe."[32] Such flattery is unwelcome because it is untrue, as
Harris explains: "The anthropocentrism that is intrinsic to every
faith cannot help appearing impossibly quaint—and therefore
impossible—given what we now know about the natural world."[33]
Says Hitchens, the atheist needs no such patronizing nonsense as
feeds the religious ego:

> Religion teaches people to be extremely self-centered and conceited.
> It assures them that god cares for them individually, and it claims
> that the cosmos was created with them specifically in mind. This
> explains the supercilious expression on the faces of those who prac-
> tice religion ostentatiously: pray excuse my modesty and humility
> but I happen to be busy on an errand from God.[34]

The issue Nietzsche takes with God's favor toward the human
species is, as usual, a step toward the radical. His complaint is not
that Christianity elevates unworthy humanity, but that it elevates
unworthy humans:

That every man, because he has an "immortal soul," is as good as every other man; that in an infinite universe of things the "salvation" of every individual may lay claim to eternal importance; that insignificant bigots and the three-fourths insane may assume that the laws of nature are constantly suspended in their behalf—it is impossible to lavish too much contempt upon such a magnification of every sort of selfishness to infinity, to insolence. And yet Christianity has to thank precisely this miserable flattery of personal vanity for its triumph—it was thus that it lured all the botched, the dissatisfied, the fallen upon evil days, the whole refuse and off-scouring of humanity to its side. . . . [O]ut of the secret nooks and crannies of bad instinct Christianity has waged a deadly war upon all feelings of reverence and distance between man and man, which is to say, upon the first prerequisite to every step upward, to every development of civilization. . . . To allow "immortality" to every Peter and Paul was the greatest, the most vicious outrage upon noble humanity ever perpetrated.[35]

Thus, whether because of the unworthiness of particular humans or humanity as a whole, this honorary elevation is received with all the disgust of an elitist toward an unaccredited honorary degree from a diploma mill.

Favor: Vanity of the Saved

What starts badly enough, as favor toward the humans of earth, poisons into favoritism toward the people of God. For example, think of how unmeritorious the Jews must have seemed to the Canaanites, their only boast as having been born in the right place at the right time. Such arrogance surely excuses the annoyance voiced by the atheist. As Harris puts it, "There is, in fact, no worldview more reprehensible in its arrogance than that of a religious believer: *the creator of the universe takes an interest in me, approves of me, loves me, and will reward me after death.*"[36] Atheist magician

Penn Jillette says simply, "Believing there's no God stops me from being solipsistic [entirely absorbed with one's self]."[37] According to Hitchens, their salvation claim is solipsistic: "How much vanity must be concealed—not too effectively at that—in order to pretend that one is the personal object of a divine plan?"[38] Says Harris, their gratitude is solipsistic: "It is time we recognized the boundless narcissism and self-deceit of the saved. It is time we acknowledged how disgraceful it is for the survivors of a catastrophe to believe themselves spared by a loving God."[39] Even the notion of sin, according to Russell, is solipsistic: "Self-importance, individual or generic, is the source of most of our religious beliefs. Even sin is a conception derived from self-importance."[40] Why even humility is solipsistic! Hitchens explains, "'There but for the grace of God,' said John Bradford in the sixteenth century, on seeing wretches led to execution, 'go I.' What this apparently compassionate observation really means—not that it really 'means' anything—is, 'There by the grace of God goes someone else.'"[41]

On the Other Hand

It is our aim now to demonstrate, respectfully and without overstatement, that the atheist basically overturns the tables he has just set up. We just observed that the atheist repudiates the concepts of submission to and special favor from a divinity. Yet consider the following passage by Russell, out of his celebrated "A Free Man's Worship": "In this lies man's true freedom: in determination to worship only the God created by our own love of the good, to respect only the heaven which inspires the insight of our best moments."[42] To thus call Russell a "worshiper" is probably a misinterpretation, yet no nonbeliever could deny that this patristic atheist was advocating some form of submission—submission not to God but to that which is created by our loftiest humanistic ideals. Similarly, the *Humanist Manifesto 2000* claims, "As humanists we urge today, as in the past, that humans not look beyond themselves for salvation. We alone are responsible for our own destiny, and the best we can do is to muster our intelligence, courage, and compassion to realize our highest aspirations."[43] Although at first this declaration appears to denounce all forms of submission, look closely, for it is truly a call *to* submission—to submit "our intelligence, courage, and compassion" to "our highest aspirations." The aim is a uniting *under* our highest aspirations. We submit not *as* the loftiest creation of God's hands but *to* the loftiest creation of ours. In other words, our freedom lies not in choosing *not* to submit so much as in choosing *what* to submit to. Submission is not the problem; rather it is to whom or to what one will submit. It is as atheist Albert Camus had his main character say in *The Fall*: "For anyone who is alone, without God and without a master, the weight of days is dreadful. Hence one must choose a master, God being out of style."[44] Submission to at least something seems essential to human nature, atheists included. It is when God enters the equation that the atheist suspects a miscalculation and fumbles for the eraser.

That the atheist advocates submission to ideals is telling enough. Yet we find an even more concrete submission being endorsed. Dawkins suggests a hypothetical:

> Whether by detecting prime numbers or by some other means, imagine that SETI does come up with unequivocal evidence of extraterrestrial intelligence, followed, perhaps, by a massive transmission of knowledge and wisdom. . . . How should we respond? A pardonable reaction would be something akin to worship, for any civilization capable of broadcasting a signal over such an immense distance is likely to be greatly superior to ours. Even if that civilization is not more advanced than ours at the time of transmission, the enormous distance between us entitles us to calculate that they must be millennia ahead of us by the time the message reaches us.[45]

47

Why is submission pardonable, necessary, perhaps even virtuous toward them but not to God? According to Dawkins, it's a matter of whether or not the object of submission exists:

> In what sense, then, would the most advanced SETI aliens not *be* gods? . . . The crucial difference between gods and god-like extraterrestrials lies not in their properties but in their provenance. Entities that are complex enough to be intelligent are products of an evolutionary process. No matter how god-like they may seem when we encounter them, they didn't start that way.[46]

But is it merely a matter of whether or not the object of submission exists? Dawkins is obviously right that a nonexistent God is unworthy of our submission. Yet do not forget the attitude displayed earlier in the chapter, that even if God *were* to exist, it would be positively immoral of him to demand such submission. Even submission accompanied by a certain worshipfulness is unproblematic in itself. It is even pardonable to submit to what has become godlike, only not to God. Submission is not the problem; God as object is.

So their repudiation of submission is half-repudiated. What about their rebuke of religious anthropocentrism? With all the sensibility and sensitivity of the big sister who reveals the nonexistence of Santa, they raise their eyebrows and say, "You knew there's nothing special about humanity, didn't you?" You are not the starlet your parents called you. Anyone who flatters you is selling something. What, then, was Russell selling in saying, "For in all things it is well to exalt the dignity of man"?[47] To witness this second reversal, one needs only refer back to all the talk of how bad submission is. Why is it so bad? It "denies human dignity, the human ego."[48] It is "quite unworthy of free men,"[49] for it denies that "every human being possesses an inherent right to be treated with respect and fairness."[50] It is "not worthy of self-respecting human beings."[51] According to Steven Weinberg, "Religion is an insult to human dignity."[52] Russell's daughter saw this inconsistency in how her father ridiculed Christians "for imagining that man is important in the vast scheme of the universe . . . yet [he] thought man and his preservation the most important thing in the world."[53]

We are not necessarily crying "Contradiction!" Just as a believer can wonder at how man is, in the words of Blaise Pascal, the "pride and refuse of the universe,"[54] the atheist can affirm man as on equal footing with his evolutionary brethren and yet worthy of special dignity. Both can be true in their own sense. The inconsistency lies in the hypocrisy of the rebuke: "How dare you call me dignified; it insults my dignity." Even the election of Christians as the special people with a special mission has its atheistic counterpart. One could argue that their name choice beats any religious self-designation in terms of grandiosity: "We [brights] are, in fact, the moral backbone of the nation: brights take their civic duties seriously precisely because they don't trust God to save humanity from its follies."[55] We are not calling atheism religious. We are merely pointing out that special favor is not the problem. Apparently we humans can recognize dignity and even bestow dignity on ourselves, but God can do neither. Again, the problem is not favor toward humanity; the problem is God as source. To sum up, atheists want neither submission to nor favor from God, even though both seem to exhaust the possibilities in dealing with a God. Moreover, since neither submission nor favor seems to be the problem, the problem must be God.

4

Death and Faith

The Lord God took the man and put him in the garden of Eden to work it and keep it. And the Lord God commanded the man, saying, "You may surely eat of every tree of the garden, but of the tree of the knowledge of good and evil you shall not eat, for in the day that you eat of it you shall surely die."

—Genesis 2:15–17

What does this ban on intelligence mean? You can do anything in this magnificent Garden, except become intelligent—the Tree of Knowledge—or immortal—the Tree of Life. What a fate God has in store for men: stupidity and mortality! A God who offers such a gift to his creatures must be perverse. . . . Let us then praise Eve who opted for intelligence at risk of death.

—Michel Onfray, *Atheist Manifesto*[1]

As it did then, the choice proves difficult today. Who is the hero? Genesis sides with God, while Michel Onfray sides with Eve. One inaccuracy, however, stacks the deck against God. It is not true, as Onfray suggests, that immortality was withheld within the garden of Eden. It was only after Eve's choice that the tree of life became off-limits. If God's purpose was to fence off both immortality and intelligence, then perhaps a case could be made for its being Christopher Hitchens's North Korea.[2] However, it was immortality inside and "intelligence" outside. Faith with immortality or death with intelligence—such was the trade. In this chapter, let us enter the mind of the atheist as he stares at the fruit, moments before choosing.

Death Is Unfair

In Albert Camus's *The Plague*, Father Paneloux points his finger at his congregation: "Calamity has come on you, my brethren, and, my brethren, you deserved it."[3] The atheist slaps the finger away. In his second sermon, after it has become clear that the plague was indiscriminately killing off even sweet children, a gentler Father Paneloux softens his voice and points up to heaven: "My brothers, the love of God is a hard love. . . . [I]t alone can reconcile us to suffering and the deaths of children, it alone can justify them, since we cannot understand them, and we can only make God's will ours."[4] The atheist agrees with the gesture but cannot stomach the tone. Whether God deals it angrily to sinners or gently to children, he is the dealer of death, and such a hand is never fair.

So the author of each life concludes each story with unresolved tragedy. Says the atheist, such a malicious author should never have been permitted to write, let alone have his writings adapted into real-life dramas. For Richard Carrier, the unthinkable is a God of disasters:

A tsunami approaches and will soon devastate the lives of millions.
A loving person warns them, and tells them how best to protect

themselves and their children. And a loving person with godlike powers could simply calm the sea, or grant everyone's bodies the power to resist serious injury, so the only tragedy they must come together to overcome is temporary pain and the loss of worldly goods. *We* would have done these things, if we could—and God can. Therefore, either God would have done them, too—or God is worse than us. Far worse. Either way, Christianity is false.[5]

Sam Harris takes on the God of diseases:

> The child born without limbs, the sightless fly, the vanished species—these are nothing less than Mother Nature caught in the act of throwing her clay. No perfect God could maintain such incongruities. It is worth remembering that if God created the world and all things in it, he created smallpox, plague, and filariasis. Any person who intentionally loosed such horrors upon the earth would be ground to dust for his crimes.[6]

Or perhaps the author of this world was not what we would traditionally consider God at all. Bertrand Russell says it is a "line which I often thought was a very plausible one—that as a matter of fact this world that we know was made by the devil at a moment when God was not looking."[7] Whatever the case, this universe of death cannot be the creation of a God of life.

Thus if God does exist, then in fighting death we find ourselves fighting God. Camus's hero Dr. Rieux could stand it no longer. After they both witnessed the agony of a child's death, Dr. Rieux shouts at the answer man Father Paneloux, "Ah! That child, anyhow, was innocent, and you know it as well as I do!" Paneloux was gentle: "I understand. That sort of thing is revolting because it passes our human understanding. But perhaps we should love what we cannot understand." The doctor shakes his head. "No, Father. I've a very different idea of love. And until my dying day I shall refuse to love a scheme of things in which children are put to torture."[8] The atheist proudly joins Rieux, who "believed himself to be on the right road, in fighting against creation as he found it."[9] In fighting against creation, they must fight against the will of its Creator, but, reasons the atheist, such a bully deserves to be fought against.

Faith Is Unreasonable

So given the choice in the garden of Eden, it seems the atheist will choose against death. But what is the alternative? Trust in God. Be content to allow him alone to know what is inside that fruit. Let go and trust. This is called faith. The problem for the atheist is that faith for him is categorized under vice, not virtue. There are at least four reasons the atheist cannot choose faith.

First, faith is said to encourage ignorance. After all, in the garden of Eden it was either faith or knowledge. Put that way, it is not difficult to guess which the atheist will choose. According to Friedrich Nietzsche, "'Faith' means the will to avoid knowing what is true."[10] In reference to the faithful, Richard Dawkins writes, "Faith (belief without evidence) is a virtue. The more your beliefs defy the evidence, the more virtuous you are."[11] According to Hitchens, faith "is a leap that has to go on and on being performed, in spite of mounting evidence to the contrary."[12] Onfray notes, "God puts to death everything that stands up to him, beginning with reason, intelligence, and the critical mind. All the rest follows in a chain reaction."[13] As if it were possible, Harris puts it even more strongly: "Every religion preaches the truth of propositions for which it has no evidence. In fact, every religion preaches the truth of propositions for which no evidence is even *conceivable*."[14] And the legions of the marching ignorant push back the champions of progress. Hitchens writes, "The argument with faith is the foundation and origin of all arguments, because it is the beginning—but not the end—of all disputes about philosophy, science, history, and human nature."[15]

Second, faith is said to encourage arrogance. After all, people of faith believe they know things no human could possibly know. According to Hitchens,

> And yet—the believers still claim to know! Not just to know, but to know *everything.* Not just to know that god exists, and that he created and supervised the whole enterprise, but also to know what "he" demands of us—from our diet to our observances to our sexual morality. . . . Such stupidity, combined with such pride, should be enough on its own to exclude "belief" from the debate. The person who is certain, and who claims divine warrant for his certainty, belongs now to the infancy of our species.[16]

Intellectually, this arrogance emerges as circular reasoning, as Harris explains: "How can any person presume to know that this is the way the universe works? Because it says so in our holy books. How do we know that our holy books are free from error? Because the books *themselves* say so."[17] Socially, the arrogance proves even less becoming, as Harris again points out: "Nothing that a Christian and a Muslim can say to each other will render their beliefs mutually vulnerable to discourse, because the very tenets of their faith have immunized them against the power of conversation. Believing strongly, without evidence, they have kicked themselves loose of the world."[18]

What happens, then, when the ignorance of the faithful mixes with their arrogance? The result is front-page fanaticism. According to Hitchens, "The nineteen suicide murderers of New York and Washington and Pennsylvania were beyond any doubt the most sincere believers on those planes. Perhaps we can hear a little less about how 'people of faith' possess moral advantages that others can only envy."[19] Harris echoes, "It is important to specify the dimension in which Muslim 'extremists' are actually extreme. They are extreme in their *faith*."[20] *Thus, the third reason the atheist cannot choose faith is that it is said to encourage fanaticism.*

Even the most patient among us would prefer any neighbor to an ignorant and arrogant one. Yet it seems the combination leads to something a bit more problematic than mere social awkwardness.

It is not our intention to argue with the atheist here. Our overriding aim is to simply allow atheists to argue against their own arguments. But in the interest of reaching a fair definition of faith, we must insert some commentary. No doubt many people of faith are ignorant, arrogant, and fanatical. However, surely these same atheists have brilliant colleagues of faith just down the hall who exhibit none of these unpleasant traits. Faith can be reasonable, humble, and peaceful; it all depends on the nature of its object. Rather than a monstrosity, faith as introduced in Genesis is merely the response of contentment to the purposeful withholding of knowledge by God to build mutual trust. By giving a prohibition, God was saying, *I will trust you to trust me*. With that, the Parent administers the first test of freedom, something necessary, as all parents know, for the eventual maturity of the child. If God had meant to imprison the human in perpetual childhood, he would never have risked the opportunity in the first place. Faith becomes necessary anytime knowledge is withheld. It becomes actual when the believer contents himself not in knowing but in knowing why he trusts God who knows. In the absence of complete certainty, the believer trusts in God because God is shown to be, whether by reason or revelation or experience, trustworthy. Far from being ignorant and arrogant, such contentment is actually quite reasonable and humble, so long as the object of that faith is trustworthy.

So the trustworthiness of God becomes the question. With faith defined less unpleasantly, is the atheist permitted to consider faith less suspiciously? It seems not, because any God who prescribes faith is held to be automatically untrustworthy. *Here we find the fourth reason the atheist cannot choose faith—namely, that he believes it is immoral of God to withhold knowledge.* Any God who would purposefully and perpetually withhold knowledge is an unfair, unfit parent whose competence is begging to be challenged. According to Dan Barker, we should have outgrown such pay-no-attention-to-the-man-behind-the-curtain parenting methods decades ago: "'Do this because I said so' is the kind of thing you say to a small child. A toddler may not be mature enough to follow a line of reasoning, so parents might have to exercise authority to prohibit something dangerous. . . . The child, in later years, should be able to obtain a reasonable explanation from the parent. If not, the parent is a petty tyrant."[21] Russell argues that absolutely no knowledge should be withheld even from children, especially in the case of sexuality:

> There is no sound reason, of any sort or kind, for concealing facts when talking to children. . . . All ignorance is regrettable, but ignorance on so important a matter as sex is a serious danger.
>
> When I say that children should be told about sex, I do not mean that they should be told only the bare physiological facts; they should be told whatever they wish to know. There should be no attempt to represent adults as more virtuous than they are, or sex as occurring only in marriage. . . . I am convinced that complete openness on sexual subjects is the best way to prevent children from thinking about them excessively, nastily, or unwholesomely, and also the almost indispensable preliminary to an enlightened sexual morality.[22]

Again, he writes, "I do not think there can be any defense for the view that knowledge is ever undesirable. I should not put barriers in the way of the acquisition of knowledge by anybody at any age."[23] After pausing again to rally for sexual freedom, he repeats, "There is no rational ground of any sort or kind for keeping a child ignorant of anything that he may wish to know, whether on sex or on any other matter."[24]

Such an overbearing curiosity begets an overturned theology. Trading Christianity for atheism, says Onfray, "will require us to set aside obedience and submission in matters of religion and to reactivate an ancient taboo: tasting the fruit of the Tree of Knowledge."[25] Again referring to sex, Russell argues, "It is ridiculous to give young people a sense of sin because they have a natural curiosity about an important matter."[26] In making it impermissible to withhold knowledge, it seems the atheist would make taboo the very making of taboos. Free at last we are—or would be but for the old faithful who hold progress back. Small wonder that atheists go beyond pitying the faithful to actually loathing faith, even calling it, as did Dawkins, "one of the world's great evils."[27] For, to them, faith restricts not only personal development but societal progress. For the faithful become not only ignorant, arrogant, fanatical victims of faith but also enforcers of despotic inhibitions.

On the Other Hand

Thus it would seem the position of the atheist is a bit dictatorial. If God is being called immoral for permitting death and prescribing faith, is not the atheist demanding immortality and limitless knowledge? However, explains the atheist, such an infinite God should be able to manage such a tall order. If God can, he should. If he is good, he owes it.

On the other hand, without God in the picture, death and faith cease to be nearly as problematic. As for the atheist's view of death, whereas he was ready to have God "ground to dust for his crimes,"[28] in the absence of God, he faces death with a dignified, almost resigned serenity. Perhaps the atheist, like Dr. Rieux, remains devoted to the prevention of deaths, but as to death in general, it is a fact to be accepted. Hitchens notes, "We are reconciled to living only once, except through our children, for whom we are perfectly happy to notice that we must make way and room."[29] Asked how he braced himself for the inescapability and finality of death, Dawkins responded, "I don't feel depressed about it. But if somebody does, that's their problem. Maybe the logic is deeply pessimistic; the universe is bleak, cold, and empty. But so what?"[30] The atheist is unafraid. According to Russell, "All fear is bad. I believe that when I die I shall rot, and nothing of my ego will survive. I am not young, and I love life. But I should scorn to shiver with terror at the thought of annihilation."[31] Condemned to the inevitable, "It remains only to cherish, ere yet the blow fall, the lofty thoughts that ennoble his little day; disdaining the coward terrors of the slave of Fate."[32] Besides, we have been there before in a sense, as David Hume noted in an interview shortly before his death: "I [James Boswell, interviewer] asked him if the thought of annihilation never gave him any uneasiness. He said not the least; no more than the thought that he had not been, as Lucretius observes."[33]

Some atheists have gone so far as to claim to prefer only one temporary life. Barker writes, "The scarcity and brevity of life is what enlarges its value. . . . If life is eternal, then life is cheap."[34] Dawkins notes, "As many atheists have said better than me, the knowledge that we have only one life should make it all the more precious."[35] Unwittingly echoing the rationale of the Christian God, Russell hints that death itself, though unpleasant, might actually be merciful. He writes, "Therefore, although it is of course a gloomy view to suppose that life will die out—at least I suppose we may say so, although sometimes when I contemplate the things that people do with their lives I think it is almost a consolation—it is not such as to render life miserable."[36] Speaking of the perpetrators of "human sacrifices, persecutions of heretics, witch-hunts, pogroms leading up to wholesale extermination by poison gases," although as always in the context of blaming God, he writes, "And can we really wish that the men who practiced them should live forever?"[37] Whatever the case, in the absence of God, death is no longer the enemy it once was.

What about godless faith? Definition here is crucial. No atheist would admit to having "belief without evidence" in, for instance, science. But this is not the approach of the thinking Christian toward God either. As we recall, faith is not inherently ignorant, arrogant, or fanatical. Biblically, it is merely trust amid the absence of complete certainty. The reasonableness or unreasonableness of faith depends on the trustworthiness of its object. Christians believe that God exists and can be trusted. Atheists believe the postulated God of Christianity to be intrinsically untrustworthy. But are there any other respectable candidates for the atheists' faith? Indeed there are.

First, many atheists call for faith in humanity. Notice Russell's use of the words *hope* and *trust*:

> A good world needs knowledge, kindliness, and courage; it does not need a regretful hankering after the past or a fettering of the free intelligence by the words uttered long ago by ignorant men. It needs a fearless outlook and a free intelligence. It needs hope for the future, not looking back all the time toward a past that is dead, which we trust will be far surpassed by the future that our intelligence can create.[38]

Similarly, note the word *believe* in the *Humanist Manifesto 2000*: "Although many problems seem intractable, we have good reasons to believe that we can marshal our best talents to solve them, and that by goodwill and dedication a better life is attainable by more and more members of the human community."[39]

Second, the atheist calls for faith in science. According to the *Humanist Manifesto II*, "Using technology wisely, we can control our environment, conquer poverty, markedly reduce disease, extend our life-span, significantly modify our behavior, alter the course of human evolution and cultural development, unlock vast new powers, and provide humankind with unparalleled opportunity for achieving an abundant and meaningful life."[40] Similarly, the *Humanist Manifesto 2000* beams, "For the first time in human history we possess the means—provided by science and technology—to ameliorate the human condition, advance happiness and freedom, and enhance human life for *all* people on the planet."[41] Russell is equally enthusiastic: "Science can teach us, and I think our own hearts can teach us, no longer to look around for imaginary supports, no longer to invent allies in the sky, but rather to look to our own efforts here below to make this world a fit place to live in, instead of the sort of place that the churches in all these centuries have made it."[42] Of course, no one is being accused of having belief *despite* evidence, neither Christian nor atheist. Both demonstrate faith as trust amid the absence of complete certainty. Yet science provides complete certainty, doesn't it? Is there really an absence of certainty needing to be filled with trust when it comes to science? There is, especially when atheists dreamily claim that scientific progress will be able to grant "an abundant and meaningful life," "ameliorate the human condition," and so on. It takes faith to believe that the ability to understand and manipulate the physical world can effect such elusive wonders.

The final candidate for faith is perhaps the most controversial, and nothing need hang on this premise. The atheist at least places faith in humanity and science, and nothing more needs to be said on the matter. However, we found this final candidate so intriguing, we had to at least mention it as a possibility. At least some atheists came across as not unfavorable toward a monistic, pantheistic deity. Chapman Cohen, onetime president of the National Secular Society in Britain, had this to say:

> It was a sound instinct that led the religious world to brand the Pantheism of Spinoza as Atheism. . . . Every intelligible Theism involves a dualism or a pluralism, while every non-theism is as inevitably driven, sooner or later, to a monism. . . . To call the monism advocated a spiritual monism does not alter the fact; it only disguises it from superficial observers and shallow thinkers. Spiritual and material are mere words. . . .

Monism—too much emphasis cannot be placed upon this truth—admits of no breaks, allows for no interference, no guidance, no special providence.[43]

According to Hitchens, a pantheistic god is far less evil than a theistic one and perhaps even harmless:

> Argument continues about whether Spinoza was an atheist: it now seems odd that we should have to argue as to whether pantheism is atheism or not. In its own express terms it is actually theistic, but Spinoza's definition of a god made manifest throughout the natural world comes very close to defining a *religious* god out of existence. And if there is a pervasive, preexisting cosmic deity, who is part of what he creates, then there is no space left for a god who intervenes in human affairs, let alone for a god who takes sides in vicious hamlet-wars between different tribes of Jews and Arabs. No text can have been written or inspired by him, for one thing, or can be the special property of one sect or tribe.[44]

Harris is perhaps the most outspoken of the atheists about the potential marriage of pantheism and atheism or at least the courtship of neuroscience and meditation:

> For millennia, contemplatives have known that ordinary people can divest themselves of the feeling that they call "I" and thereby relinquish the sense that they are separate from the rest of the universe. This phenomenon, which has been reported by practitioners in many spiritual traditions, is supported by a wealth of evidence— neuroscientific, philosophical, and introspective. Such experiences are "spiritual" or "mystical," for want of better words, in that they are relatively rare (unnecessarily so), significant (in that they uncover genuine facts about the world), and personally transformative.[45]

Clearly many atheists, including Hitchens, have been outspokenly critical of Eastern religious practices. Yet Spinoza-brand pantheism gets a special exemption. Why? It cannot be that it requires no faith—of course this brand of spirituality requires a certain trust due to the absence of complete certainty. An atheist sympathetic to pantheism might respond that what gives it special exemption is that its claims might be more experientially verified, whereas Christian faith, for example, has to lean more heavily on historical and philosophical reasoning. C. S. Lewis proposes his own explanation for its attraction: "The Pantheist's God does nothing, demands nothing. He is there if you wish for him, like a book on a shelf. He will not pursue you. There is no danger that at any time heaven and earth should flee away at His glance."[46] One thing is for sure: it certainly boosts credibility to posthumously enlist intellects like Spinoza and Einstein for the cause of atheism.

Let us summarize. When viewed within the Christian system, death is unspeakably evil, a divine crime worth being "ground to dust" over.[47] Likewise, faith within the Christian system is ignorant, arrogant, and fanatical. So neither of the garden of Eden varieties is edible. However, out from underneath God, death is natural and nothing to fret over. It is fine so long as it is dealt by life but inexcusable when decreed by God. Moreover, faith is understandable, even virtuous, when the object is something trustworthy like man and science. Thus, the problem with death and faith lies not in themselves but in their utilization by God. Once again the problem is God.

Like a blocked basketball shot, death upsets our aims. "Foul!" cries the atheist. Like a referee's controversial call, faith demands trust. "Boo!" cries the atheist. Neither death nor faith as given by God agrees with the atheist. Yet the choice between binding oneself *to* the Source of life and loosing oneself *from* the Source of life seems to exhaust the possibilities of a theistic universe. How would the atheist have chosen in the garden of Eden? There is a way to escape a seemingly insurmountable dilemma, and that is with a counterdilemma. We imagine that the atheist will likely refuse both options as proposed by God in favor of a restatement of the dilemma. It will be recalled that, in the garden of Eden, it was Satan that recast the choice in fresh terms. It was never faith versus death, explains Satan, but merely ignorance versus knowledge. "You will not surely die. For God knows that when you eat of it your eyes will be opened, and you will be like God, knowing good and evil" (Gen. 3:4b–5). "Well, when you put it that way . . . ," says the atheist. And ever since, faith, for the un-believing, has become synonymous with the chains of ignorance. As Barker puts it, "The bible says that the '*ungodly* are like chaff which the wind blows away' (Ps. 1:4). That's fine with me. I prefer the winds of freethought to the chains of orthodoxy."[48] Hence the choice becomes obvious, thanks to the new perspective. Christian faith minus God is utter ignorance, while death minus God means a lifetime of freedom. In the passage that follows, Onfray's words might chill the believer, but then again, for the atheist, God is the enemy. And the enemy of my enemy is . . .

> Satan—"the adversary, the accuser"—breathes the wind of free-dom across the dirty waters of the primal world where obedience reigns supreme—the reign of maximum servitude. Beyond good and evil, and not simply as an incarnation of the latter, the devil talks libertarian possibilities into being. He restores to men their power over themselves and the world, frees them from supervision and control. We may rightly conclude that these fallen angels at-tract the hatred of monotheisms. On the other hand, they attract the incandescent love of atheists.[49]

Guilt and Rules

When the natural consequences of an act are no longer "natural," but are regarded as produced by the ghostly creations of superstition—by "God," by "spirits," by "souls"—and reckoned as merely "moral" consequences, as rewards, as punishments, as hints, as lessons, then the whole ground-work of knowledge is destroyed—then the greatest of crimes against humanity has been perpetrated.—I repeat that sin, man's self-desecration par excellence, was invented in order to make science, culture, and every elevation and ennobling of man impossible; the priest rules through the invention of sin.

—Friedrich Nietzsche, *The Antichrist*[1]

The link between God and morality seems to be a crucial, if not a touchy, issue for atheists. Invariably, when the atheist is asked if unbelief absolves blame and excuses licentiousness, the atheist immediately spins the question back on the questioner. After all, do you not know that it is religious people responsible for the great injustices in the world? In fact, to even suggest that God is necessary for morality is to admit to needing supervision for an overabundance of depravity. Instead of tackling the issue of moral ontology head-on, Richard Dawkins begins his chapter "The Roots of Morality: Why Are We Good?" by quoting hate mail from religious nutcases that spew (original spelling intact), "Hello, cheese-eating scumbags. Their [sic] are way more of us Christians than you losers. Their [sic] is no separation of church and state and you heathens will lose."[2] Similarly, in a chapter "Does Religion Make People Behave Better?," Christopher Hitchens claims for secularism the truly great deeds of history, such as those by Dr. Martin Luther King Jr. and Abraham Lincoln, while equating truly religiously motivated action with such horrors as Rwandan slaughters and child soldiers.[3] It seems a bit tilted, does it not?

The question of moral ontology is supposed to be settled by Hitchens's following anecdote. In light of his atheism, A. J. Ayer is told, "Then I cannot see why you do not lead a life of unbridled immorality," to which Ayer responds, "I must say that I think that is a perfectly monstrous insinuation."[4] That is not an argument but an evasion! At the very least, it pushes the question back a step, for the atheist declares that humans are good because they have the capacity within. And that universal, innate quality is supposed to prove there is no God? Even the suggestion that this intrinsic objectivity comes from God is immediately ridiculed on the basis that "religious people do bad things." Back at you, says Emma Goldman: "Do not all theists insist that there can be no morality, no justice, honesty, or fidelity without the belief in a Divine Power? Based upon fear and hope, such morality has always been a vile product, imbued partly with self-righteousness, partly with hypocrisy."[5] Now, to be fair, there have been attempted atheistic explanations of moral ontology (e.g., Harris's *The Moral Landscape*). But the typical evasive cheap shot hints that the atheist prefers side issues over debating the possibility of a connection.

We write all this to make clear how imperative it is to the atheist to prevent God from being linked with morality. At the mere insinuation of a connection, the atheist begins listing religious crimes. We are in a chapter on guilt and rules. Because the atheist severs all relation between God and what he considers to be any intelligent morality, he will also declare freedom from all guilt and rules issuing from such a superfluous God. So given the only two possible responses to a moral God—obey the rules or reap the guilt—we can expect the atheist to respond, "Neither."

It Wasn't My Fault: Guilt Presupposes Responsibility

The first problem the atheist has with guilt under God is that it presupposes responsibility. Such an assumption is prescientific, as Sam Harris explains:

> We know, for instance, that no human being creates his own genes or his early life experiences, and yet most of us believe that these factors determine his character throughout life. It seems true enough to say that the men and women on death row either have bad genes, bad parents, bad ideas, or bad luck. Which of these quantities are they responsible for?[6]

Labeling someone as guilty is as unfair as blaming someone for a genetic disease, says Bertrand Russell:

> It is evident that a man with a propensity to crime must be stopped, but so must a man who has hydrophobia and wants to bite people, although nobody considers him morally responsible. A man who is suffering from plague has to be imprisoned until he is cured, although nobody thinks him wicked. The same thing should be done with a man who suffers from a propensity to commit forgery; but there should be no more idea of guilt in the one case than in the other.[7]

After all, a man's "annoying behavior is a result of antecedent causes which, if you follow them long enough, will take you beyond the moment of his birth and therefore to events for which he cannot be held responsible by any stretch of imagination."[8] Thus, "It is no longer Satan who makes sin but bad glands and unwise conditioning."[9] Michel Onfray goes so far as to say, "This collusion between the principle of free will and the voluntary choice of evil over good—which legitimizes the notion of responsibility, and therefore guilt, and therefore punishment—requires the workings of magical thinking."[10]

With the abolition of guilt comes our long-awaited emancipation from the nasty doctrine of sin. Dan Barker sounds the proclamation:

> We atheists possess "salvation" not because we are released from a sentence, but because we don't deserve the punishment in the first place. We have committed no "sin." Sin is a religious concept, and in some religions salvation is the deliverance from the "wages of sin"—which is death or eternal punishment. Sin has been defined as "missing the mark" of God's expectations or holiness, or "offending God," so it follows that since there is no god, there is no sin, therefore no need of salvation. How much respect should you have for a doctor who cuts you with a knife in order to sell you a bandage? Only those who consider themselves sinners need this kind of deliverance—it is a religious solution to a religious problem.[11]

Thus Barker can say, "If salvation is the cure, then atheism is the prevention."[12] Those who cling to the old slavery days must have some investment in the trade, according to Russell: "The view that criminals are 'wicked' and 'deserve' punishment is not one which a rational morality can support. . . . The vindictive feeling called 'moral indignation' is merely a form of cruelty."[13]

It's My Life: Guilt Disrespects Humanity

The second problem with guilt under God is that guilt insults human dignity. Ludwig Feuerbach describes Christianity's depressing anthropology: "Religion further denies goodness as a quality of human nature; man is wicked, corrupt, incapable of good; but, on the other hand, God is only good—the Good Being."[14] Barker adds, "The biblical view of human nature is negative. Humans don't deserve respect; they deserve damnation. We are all tainted with Original Sin."[15] The problem with such a self-image is obvious, as Hitchens voices: "How much self-respect must be sacrificed in order that one may squirm continually in awareness of one's own sin?"[16] Add to that Nietzsche's typical charm: "Christianity finds sickness necessary, just as the Greek spirit had need of a superabundance of health—the actual ulterior purpose of the whole system of salvation of the church is to make people ill."[17] Yet what if Christianity were to promise to absolve sinners of their guilt? No good, explains Barker, because it fails to absolve sinners of having been sinners:

> Suppose you were convicted of a horrible crime and sentenced to life in prison, but after a few years behind bars you are surprised to hear you are being released. This "salvation" would be a wonderful experience. But which would make you feel better: learning you were released because you were pardoned by the good graces of the governor, or because you were found to be innocent of the crime? Which would give you more dignity?[18]

You Hate Me: Guilt Promotes Cruelty

The third problem the atheist has with the Christian doctrine of guilt is that it both proves cruelty in God and promotes cruelty in man. To the atheist, God is the insecure school principal who enjoys calling schoolchildren into his office and watching them squirm under his scowl. This mandatory and ongoing viewing of one's past sins is meant to be a knife turning that draws shrieks of repentance. Russell puts it simply: "Kindness is inhibited by the belief in sin and punishment."[19] Far from being a means by which the sinner is made well, guilt is a means of turning a well man into a sinner. Such a reversal transforms sincere people into cruel people with a cruel God. According to Russell, "The conception of Sin which is bound up with Christian ethics is one that does an extraordinary amount of harm, since it affords people an outlet for their sadism which they believe to be legitimate, and even noble."[20] When taught to the young, the doctrine of guilt violates the innocence of childhood with loathsome self-images. Still recovering from government-funded Christian indoctrination in school, Hitchens half-wishes that "[t]hose who preached hatred and fear and guilt and who ruined innumerable childhoods should have been thankful that the hell they preached was one among their wicked falsifications, and that they were not sent to rot there."[21] As a former member of the headmaster's faculty, former evangelist Barker would know: "What worse psychological damage could be done to children than to tell them that they basically are no good? What does this do to self-image?"[22] Moreover, says Russell, such a costly doctrine boasts no advantages: "The sense of sin which dominates many children and young people and often lasts on into later life is a misery and a source of distortion that serves no useful purpose of any sort or kind."[23]

How then, it might be asked, can we expect people to change from their wickedness, unless from realization of guilt? Such a question assumes too much, argues Russell. Start as early as possible. All that is needed for a child to be delivered from true vice is rather simple:

A child must feel himself the object of warm affection on the part of some at least of the adults with whom he has to do, and he must not be thwarted in his natural activities and curiosities except when danger to life or health is concerned. In particular, there must be no taboo on sex knowledge, or on conversation about matters which conventional people consider improper. If these simple precepts are observed from the start, the child will be fearless and friendly.[24]

No sweat at all—and no trembling. Love, not cruelty, begets love.

Rules: The Problem We Shouldn't Have

The natural solution for the atheist who hates the notion of feeling guilt under God would be for the atheist to simply obey the rules prescribed by God. It is as straightforward as the most elementary parent-child agreement: if you do not want the guilt, do not disobey the rules. However, rules from God are just as problematic for the atheist as guilt; three reasons are given. First, would it not be the Creator's fault in the first place that we would need so many rules? The need for rules is a problem we should never have had in the first place. Why work to remove the problem caused by God; why not simply remove God and watch the problem evaporate? Recall Barker's axiom: "If salvation is the cure, then atheism is the prevention."[25] Why incriminate oneself with such a burden? Believing in such a God is requesting a family doctor who cripples you to sell you crutches or poisons you to keep filling your prescription. Recall the question as put by Carl Sagan: "Why is there such a long list of things that God tells people to do? Why didn't God do it right in the first place?"[26] Hitchens puts it simply: "Nothing could be sillier than having a 'maker' who then forbade the very same instinct he instilled."[27] It turns out that even after granting that God can somehow be excused for such a flagrant structural flaw, two additional observations make the problem of rules insurmountable.

Rules: The Solution We Never Needed

According to atheists, morality can be divided into two categories. We might call these "scientific" morality and "superstitious" morality. As Russell explains, "Modern morals are a mixture of two elements: on the one hand, rational precepts as to how to live together peaceably in a society, and on the other hand traditional taboos derived originally from some ancient superstition, but proximately from sacred books."[28] Elsewhere, Russell restates the categories: "Moral rules are broadly of two kinds: there are those which have no basis except in a religious creed, and there are those which have an obvious basis in social utility."[29] Thus, it is laughably simplistic to credit religion, let alone one religion, with being the source of all morality, says Harris: "The pervasive idea that religion is somehow the *source* of our deepest ethical intuitions is absurd. We no more get our sense that cruelty is wrong from the pages of the Bible than we get our sense that two plus two equals four from the pages of a textbook on mathematics."[30] The assumption is that true morality, like mathematics, is discoverable by rationality. Any additional morality is irrational and must be left behind as knowledge rolls on. As Russell puts it,

> It is evident that a man with a scientific outlook on life cannot let himself be intimidated by texts of Scripture or by the teaching of the church. He will not be content to say "such-and-such an act is sinful, and that ends the matter." He will inquire whether it does any harm or whether, on the contrary, the belief that it is sinful does harm. And he will find that, especially in what concerns sex, our current morality contains a very great deal of which the origin is purely superstitious.[31]

Such an evaluation and dismissal must be made when scientific man comes upon superstitious morality. What happens when superstitious man stumbles upon scientific morality? God cannot suddenly step up and claim credit, according to Hitchens: "I can think of a handful of priests and bishops and rabbis and imams who have put humanity ahead of their own sect or creed. . . . But this is a compliment to humanism, not to religion."[32]

Thus we come to the second reason that rules under God are problematic. That morality which is undiscoverable by human reason, which can truly be said to come from God or at least religion, is unhelpful at best. It is the solution we never needed. Superstitious, superfluous morality is defined as such by at least four criteria.

First, superstitious morality impedes pleasure. In other words, it obstructs sex. Hitchens laments, "Almost every sexual impulse has been made the occasion for prohibition, guilt, and shame."[33] According to Russell, "The worst feature of the Christian religion, however, is its attitude toward sex."[34] Harris softens the tone for reasoning to Christian parents: "Your efforts to constrain the sexual behavior of consenting adults—and even to discourage your own sons and daughters from having premarital sex—are almost never geared toward the relief of human suffering."[35] According to Dawkins, the "single fiercely unpleasant God" of the three monotheisms is "morbidly obsessed with sexual restrictions."[36] In place of the old taboos, we should prescribe an eyes-on-your-own-paper policy. Dawkins imagines an "amended Ten Commandments," of which one rule becomes, "Enjoy your own sex life (so long as it damages nobody else) and leave others to enjoy theirs in private whatever their inclinations, which are none of your business."[37] The *Humanist Manifesto II* explains, "The many varieties of sexual exploration should not in themselves be considered 'evil.'"[38]

Second, superstitious morality enforces pain. The clergyman doubles as sexual referee, not merely blowing the whistle on pleasure but being a homeboy who allows the pious side to plow over the other team. After all, according to Harris, "Anyone who believes that God is watching us from beyond the stars will feel that punishing peaceful men and women for their private pleasure is perfectly reasonable."[39] Russell blows the whistle on the referees for a double violation:

Clergymen almost necessarily fail in two ways as teachers of morals. They condemn acts which do no harm and they condone acts which do great harm. They all condemn sexual relations between unmarried people who are fond of each other but not yet sure that they wish to live together all their lives. Most of them condemn birth control. None of them condemn the brutality of a husband who causes his wife to die of too frequent pregnancies.[40]

The clergy having chronically misused their authority, their infallible pronouncements on modern sexual ethics can be dismissed as toxic remedies millennia out of date. Hitchens explains, "Very importantly, the divorce between the sexual life and fear, and the sexual life and disease, and the sexual life and tyranny, can now at last be attempted, on the sole condition that we banish all religions from the discourse."[41] According to the *Humanist Manifesto II*, "In the area of sexuality, we believe that intolerant attitudes, often cultivated by orthodox religions and puritanical cultures, unduly repress sexual conduct. The right to birth control, abortion, and divorce should be recognized."[42] After widening the shield to cover "in vitro fertilization, surrogate motherhood, genetic engineering, organ transplantation, and cloning," the *Humanist Manifesto 2000* declares, "We cannot look back to the moral absolutes of the past for guidance here. We need to respect autonomy of choice."[43]

Third, superstitious morality exceeds practicality. Many of God's rules aim for the heart, as if behavioral modification were not invasive enough. Not content to oversee the bedroom, God demands entry into the mind. Intrusiveness aside, such commands ask the practically impossible. On the one hand, God prohibits the inevitable. Hitchens explains,

> Finally, instead of the condemnation of evil actions, there is an oddly phrased condemnation of impure thoughts. . . . [I]t demands the impossible: a recurrent problem with all religious edicts. One may be forcibly restrained from worked actions, or barred from committing them, but to forbid people from *contemplating* them is too

much. . . . If god really wanted people to be free of such thoughts, he should have taken more care to invent a different species.[44]

Such meddling has its counterpart in the political world, according to Hitchens. Referencing God's covetousness and lust prohibitions, he presents an analogy: "To the totalitarian edicts that begin with revelation from absolute authority, and that are enforced by fear, and based on a sin that had been committed long ago, are added regulations that are often immoral and impossible at the same time. The essential principle of totalitarianism is to make laws that are *impossible to obey*."[45] Thus, not only does God prohibit the inevitable, but he also commands the impossible. Worst of all, he commands love, something akin to forcing kids to not merely eat their vegetables but to enjoy them. According to Barker, "Love can't be commanded. No one has the right to tell me to love someone else."[46] To Hitchens, such expectations defy our fundamental constitution:

> The order to "love thy neighbor *as thyself* " is too extreme and too strenuous to be obeyed, as is the hard-to-interpret instruction to love others "as I have loved you." Humans are not so constituted as to care for others as much as themselves: the thing simply cannot be done (as any intelligent "creator" would well understand from studying his own design). Urging humans to be superhumans, on pain of death and torture, is the urging of terrible self-abasement at their repeated and inevitable failure to keep the rules.[47]

Any parent who prohibits the inevitable and commands the impossible is asking for rebellion, and the atheist obliges.

Fourth, superstitious morality commands piety, something which, according to atheists, has absolutely nothing to contribute to true morality. No gods, no idols, no blasphemy, no Sabbath skipping—Harris exposes the "vertical" section of the Ten Commandments: "The first four injunctions have nothing whatsoever to do with morality."[48] Sabbath breaking, idolatry, and sorcery are just a few of a "wide variety of other imaginary crimes."[49] Now, to the believer, severing God from morality is like barring a teacher from the classroom, but no problem arises as the atheist defines morality. It is because Harris declares that "[q]uestions of morality are questions about happiness and suffering" that he can say, "This is why you and I do not have moral obligations toward rocks."[50] Perhaps not, but the implication is unmistakable; since morality deals only in pleasure and pain, we have no more obligation toward God than toward rocks. Because only immorality with a flesh-and-blood victim is immoral, criminal activity will plummet as the definition of crime is tweaked. Harris explains, "Behaviors like drug use, prostitution, sodomy, and the viewing of obscene materials have been categorized as 'victimless crimes.'"[51] However, "The idea of a victimless crime is nothing more than a judicial reprise of the Christian notion of sin."[52] After all, the Christian views each crime as a slap in God's face. After morality's redefinition, such a gesture merely slaps the air. Says Harris, "It is time we realized that crimes without victims are like debts without creditors."[53]

Rules: The Solution We Already Had

First, rules under God are the problem we never should have had; if God had created us better, any rules would be unnecessary. Second, superstitious morality is the solution we never needed; it prescribes such spiteful superfluities as impeding pleasure, enforcing pain, exceeding practicality, and commanding piety. If God were a doctor, the first problem is that he cripples you and sells you crutches. The second problem is that he prescribes expensive placebos that induce vomiting and deaden sexual vivaciousness. In keeping with the analogy, the third problem with rules under God is that he repackages legitimate medicines under his own name and hikes the prices. In other words, God plagiarizes the learned wisdom of the great moralists and inserts the occasional "Thou shalt not" to elude the plagiarism spotters. Whereas superstitious morality is the solution we never needed, scientific morality is the solution we already had.

So what is this solution we already had? Let us ask perhaps the most revered name among atheists, Charles Darwin. According to Darwin, the solution evolved as naturally as we did:

> A man who has no assured and ever present belief in the existence of a personal God or of a future existence with retribution and reward, can have for his rule of life, as far as I can see, only to follow those impulses and instincts which are the strongest or which seem to him the best ones. A dog acts in this manner, but he does so blindly. A man, on the other hand, looks forwards and backwards, and compares his various feelings, desires and recollections. He then finds, in accordance with the verdict of all the wisest men that the highest satisfaction is derived from following certain impulses, namely the social instincts. If he acts for the good of others, he will receive the approbation of his fellow men and gain the love of those with whom he lives; and this latter gain undoubtedly is the highest pleasure on this earth.[54]

In the atheist's mind, to credit such a natural process to the scribbling of God on a stone tablet is an insult to nature akin to reducing the beauty of the crescent moon to God's thumbnail. Nature taught us right and wrong, truths that religions hijacked for their own moralities. Dawkins suggests, "And if we have independent criteria for choosing among religious moralities, why not cut out the middle man and go straight for the moral choice without the religion?"[55] Not only is the real manufacturer insulted when religion sticks morality with a "Made in Heaven" sticker, but so are we. Says Hitchens, "It is surely insulting to the people of Moses to imagine they had come this far under the impression that murder, adultery, theft, and perjury were permissible."[56] Our morality never needed divine authorship for legitimacy; much less did it need all the unpalatable embellishments the Author chose to add. According to Harris, "Jesus clearly tells us that love can transform human life. We need not believe that he was born of a virgin or will be returning to earth as a superhero to take these teachings to heart."[57] Not only does the atheist locate much excess to Christian morality but also much of importance that is left out as well. As Hitchens puts it, "Then there is the very salient question of what the commandments do *not* say. Is it too modern to notice that there is nothing about the protection of children from cruelty, nothing about rape, nothing about slavery, and nothing about genocide?"[58] Put mildly, any morality that counts, we already had or are fully capable of discovering.

From what we have seen, it appears the atheist has the mysterious ability to weed through traditional Christian morality to the heart of Christianity itself. The atheist can mine beneath the layers of cultural taboos and magical embellishments to truly timeless gems of morality. We all know we should love one another, and so on. In this sense, it almost seems as though the atheist can be more Christian than can Christians who insist that the beautiful must remain unearthed beneath the dusty layers of tradition. Perhaps this is why Nietzsche seems to have been silently disowned by many of today's atheists (the rogue if not anarchic Onfray being a notable exception). To Nietzsche, those gems central to the Christian faith were trash. In *Thus Spake Zarathustra*, Nietzsche describes three metamorphoses for the liberation of the human spirit—from spirit to camel, from camel to lion, and from lion to child. The transition to camel is unfortunate due to the burdens the human spirit carries. The second is a liberating metamorphosis:

> In the loneliest desert, however, the second metamorphosis occurs: here the spirit becomes a lion who would conquer his freedom and be master in his own desert. Here he seeks out his last master: he wants to fight him and his last god; for ultimate victory he wants to fight with the great dragon.

Who is the great dragon whom the spirit will no longer call lord and god? "Thou shalt" is the name of the great dragon. But the spirit of the lion says, "I will."[59]

With the dragon slain, and "values, thousands of years old" overturned, fresh values await birth. Thus, the lion becomes a child, for "[t]he child is innocence and forgetting, a new beginning, a game, a self-propelled wheel, a first movement, a sacred 'Yes.'"[60]

Today's gospel presentation is crafted flawlessly: There is now nothing holding you back from becoming an atheist. Culture's most cherished Christian values are not only compatible with but resultant from atheism. Not so fast, says Nietzsche. Nietzsche was not calling for three metamorphoses in order to emerge as basically the same creature. Instead, he proposed radically new morality, shocking even unbelievers with quips such as, "Man should be educated for war, and woman for the recreation of the warrior; all else is folly."[61] Perhaps his contempt for women and the "bungled and botched" would never earn Dawkins's stamp of approval as "stunningly elegant," but what does that matter? What matters is not whether today's atheist can agree with but whether he can argue against Nietzsche. Even as esteemed an atheist as Russell would like to but cannot. Russell can suggest what Buddha or Jesus might say against Nietzsche, but anything more is a step further than Russell's epistemology warrants:

> But I do not know how to prove that [Buddha] is right by any argument such as can be used in a mathematical or a scientific question. I dislike Nietzsche because he likes the contemplation of pain, because he erects conceit into a duty, because the men whom he most admires are conquerors, whose glory is cleverness in causing men to die. But I think the ultimate argument against his philosophy, as against any unpleasant but internally self-consistent ethic, lies not in an appeal to facts, but in an appeal to the emotions. Nietzsche despises universal love: I feel it the motive power to all that I desire

as regards the world. His followers have had their innings, but we may hope that it is coming rapidly to an end.[62]

In the end, Russell can offer us no argument more substantial than an appeal to dislikes, emotion, and hope. The atheist says we can discover a rational morality without any help from above. Perhaps theoretically we can, but whose version of morality ends up going down in history? Russell's emotional appeal squeaks back at Nietzsche's war cry. And optimism tries to reconcile its miscalculations with a bloody century.

And One More Thing

To review, guilt under God is problematic because it presupposes responsibility, disrespects humanity, and promotes cruelty. Rules under God are problematic because they point to a God who should have created us better and because they can be divided into rules that are either completely unnecessary or for which God is completely unnecessary. A final objection to guilt and rules can be voiced. It is the final inch before the door slams decisively shut and the "No gods allowed!" sign is hung. The objection is this: Why does God care about such petty things in the first place? Only a God who respects privacy is worth respecting. Onfray narrates the problem: "God was not content with that one prohibition on the forbidden fruit. Ever since, he has revealed himself to us only through taboos. The monotheistic religions live exclusively by prescriptions and constraints: things to do and things not to do, to say and not to say, think and not to think, perform and not to perform."[63] We can easily imagine a more respectable God, says Dawkins: "Compared with the Old Testament's psychotic delinquent, the deist God of the eighteenth-century Enlightenment is an altogether grander being: worthy of his cosmic creation, loftily unconcerned with human affairs, sublimely aloof from our private thoughts and hopes, caring nothing for our messy sins or mumbled contritions."[64]

Moreover, a petty God creates petty subjects. Apparently, Saint Augustine still has atoning to do for his theft of the pears, except the problem is no longer the crime, but the idiocy of his repentance. Surely he should have known that if God is indeed God, he would not have given a thought to such a boys-being-boys trifle. According to Dawkins, such self-deprecation is dangerous but common:

> Augustine's pronouncements and debates epitomize, for me, the unhealthy preoccupation of early Christian theologians with sin. They could have devoted their pages and their sermons to extolling the sky splashed with stars, or mountains and green forests, seas and dawn choruses. These are occasionally mentioned, but the Christian focus is overwhelmingly on sin sin sin sin sin sin sin. What a nasty little preoccupation to have dominating your life.[65]

What arrogant humility, thinks Hitchens: "Augustine was a self-centered fantasist and an earth-centered ignoramus: he was guiltily convinced that god cared about his trivial theft from some unimportant pear trees, and quite persuaded—by an analogous solipsism—that the sun revolved around the earth."[66] Does God have such a small kingdom that he insists on turning every molehill into a mountain? Dawkins exclaims, "Why should a divine being, with creation and eternity on his mind, care a fig for petty human malefactions? We humans give ourselves such airs, even aggrandizing our poky little 'sins' to the level of cosmic significance!"[67] A God who insists on being invited into each triviality is seen as a busybody who must not have much of anything important to do.

On the Other Hand

Yet it must not be assumed that since the atheist repudiates guilt and rules under God that the atheist repudiates guilt and rules. It may appear that obedience to his rules and guilt from disobedience of his rules are the only two possible ways of relating to such a God. They are not. The atheist opts for a third option: disregard. He pulls out of the relationship. But must the atheist who falls from heaven seek to create hell on earth? Must he be a shameless, lawless reprobate?

First, the atheist is not anti-guilt, just anti-God. Admittedly, Hitchens was no saint, but he welcomed appropriate guilt as only healthy:

> If I was suspected of raping a child, or torturing a child, or infecting a child with venereal disease, or selling a child into sexual or any other kind of slavery, I might consider committing suicide whether I was guilty or not. If I had actually committed the offense, I would welcome death in any form that it might take. This revulsion is innate in any healthy person, and does not need to be taught.[68]

It is only fair that each person bears responsibility for his own actions, as Hitchens makes clear in reference to Christ's atonement: "I can pay your debt. . . . But I cannot absolve you of your responsibilities. It would be immoral of me to offer, and immoral of you to accept."[69] Russell admits that at least the majority of humanity needs a measure of repentance:

> Except for those rare spirits that are born without sin, there is a cavern of darkness to be traversed before that temple can be entered. The gate of the cavern is despair, and its floor is paved with the gravestones of abandoned hopes. There self must die; there the eagerness, the greed of untamed desire, must be slain, for only so can the soul be freed from the empire of Fate. But out of the cavern, the Gate of Renunciation leads again to the daylight of freedom, by whose radiance a new insight, a new joy, a new tenderness, shine forth to gladden the pilgrim's heart.[70]

Even the atheist who boasts of having absolutely no sin to feel guilty over would shoulder the guilt if appropriate. Note Barker's hypothetical humility in the midst of what appears to be arrogance: "I don't have any sins, but if I did, I wouldn't want Jesus to die for my sins. I would say, 'No, thanks. I will take responsibility for my own actions.'"[71] Again, where appropriate, guilt is necessary. The one type of guilt that they know is never appropriate is guilt under God.

Likewise, atheists are not anti-rules. Even the radical Nietzsche never called for the abolition of rules but for their emancipation from Christianity. The human spirit is not to remain the lion destroyer, but to transform into the child creator. As long as the child is enjoying himself and not hurting anyone, why wag your finger at him? At the risk of sounding simplistic, it seems that is the sum of the atheist's morality. Russell suggests, "What we have to do positively is to ask ourselves what moral rules are most likely to promote human happiness."[72] Certain virtues are thus naturally elevated, as Russell illustrates: "As to morality, a great deal depends on how one understands that term. For my part, I think the important virtues are kindness and intelligence."[73] Inevitably, with the elevation of some, other traditional virtues begin to slide toward vice, as Russell continues: "Intelligence is impeded by any creed, no matter what; and kindness is inhibited by the belief in sin and punishment."[74] In fact, it turns out the primary trouble with religious morality is that it gets in the way of human happiness. Russell explains, "It is not only intellectually but also morally that religion is pernicious. I mean by this that it teaches ethical codes which are not conducive to human happiness."[75] Instead, "It has chosen to label as morality a certain narrow set of rules of conduct which have nothing to do with human happiness; and when you say that this or that ought to be done because it would make for human happiness, they think that has nothing to do with the matter at all."[76]

It is clear, then, why the atheist has such revulsion to connecting God with morality. It insults him. It challenges the claim he has built his life on, that he is able to be moral but not godly. In fact, the atheist claims to be moral *because* he is ungodly. It is not just that atheists do not want God's guilt or rules; they believe they do not need them. Free to define morality, they become the most moral beings that exist—natural or supernatural. It is an odd request for no guilt and no rules except those not given by God. Yet there it is: We want neither obedience to his rules nor its opposite, guilt. Is this not an impossible demand? No, simply remove God, and all is right with the world.

6

Punishment and Pardon

New Testament theology adds a new injustice, topped off by a new sadomasochism whose viciousness even the Old Testament barely exceeds. It is, when you think about it, remarkable that a religion should adopt an instrument of torture and execution as its sacred symbol, often worn around the neck.

—Richard Dawkins, *The God Delusion*[1]

A recovery of the old sense of sin is essential to Christianity. Christ takes it for granted that men are bad. Until we feel this assumption of His to be true, though we are part of the world He came to save, we are not part of the audience to whom His words are addressed.

—C. S. Lewis, *The Problem of Pain*[2]

Like Martin Luther, the atheist pounds on the door of heaven and demands freedom from injustices. We have discussed six grievances thus far: submission and favor, death and faith, guilt and rules. Unlike Luther, the atheist may call for reformation but cannot seriously hope for it. As the Bible says, God is unchanging. Release from these perceived injustices comes only after emancipation from God; that is the only way. Now we arrive at two injustices that are very likely to be to the atheist what the practice of indulgences was to Luther. We come to what might easily have been the cause of the atheist's first or primary revulsion—not with the world but with God himself. We are referring to the passages in the Bible that made them wince. It was reading the Bible from cover to cover that served as Richard Carrier's confirmation in the unfaith. He says, "When I finished the last page, though alone in my room, I declared aloud, 'Yep, I'm an atheist.'"[3] This chapter allows the atheist to comment on those passages that first forced his misgivings about God's character. He is a punisher and, only in that dark context, a pardoner of some.

Unrighteous Anger: God as Punisher

The history of atheism could be traced through famous atheists or through the various philosophical stages of atheism. Perhaps it would be interesting to trace the history of atheism through the atheists' attempts at devising the greatest one-line insult to God. Much like preteen boys trading ever-escalating smack talk, it is a competition in which the point is to prove "I can do better than that." Let us start with deist Thomas Jefferson's description of God as "a being of terrific character—cruel, vindictive, capricious, and unjust,"[4] a description that makes Jefferson's indictments of King George in the American Declaration of Independence look quite restrained. Jefferson's friend Thomas Paine felt he could do better: "Whenever we read the obscene stories, the voluptuous debaucheries, the cruel and torturous executions, the unrelenting vindictiveness, with which more than half the Bible is filled, it would be more consistent that we called it the word of a demon, than the word of God."[5] Perhaps Charles Darwin's wife's devoutness helped to tame him out of the running; to Darwin, the Old Testament's God is merely a "revengeful tyrant."[6] Sam Harris adds, "A close study of our holy books reveals that the God of Abraham is a ridiculous fellow—capricious, petulant, and cruel—and one with whom a covenant is little guarantee of health or happiness."[7] To further pack the punch, he adds, "If these are the characteristics of God, then the worst among us have been created far more in his image than we ever could have hoped."[8] Dan Barker scores votes in our anti-bullying culture with, "Having to spend eternity pretending to worship a petty tyrant who tortures those who insult his authority would be more hellish than baking in eternal flames. There is no way such a bully can earn my admiration."[9] Nonetheless, Richard Dawkins probably wins, unless excessive thesaurus consultation is grounds for disqualification: "The God of the Old Testament is arguably the most unpleasant character in all fiction: jealous and proud of it; a petty, unjust, unforgiving control-freak; a vindictive, bloodthirsty ethnic cleanser; a misogynistic, homophobic, racist, infanticidal, genocidal, filicidal, pestilential, megalomaniacal, sadomasochistic, capriciously malevolent bully."[10] One wonders if these atheists are trying more to shock believers, embolden unbelievers, or simply vent. Whatever the case, their point is clear: A judgmental God deserves judgment; he should be treated as he wants us to be treated.

After all, the Bible as they read it presents a God with all the humbug of Scrooge mixed with the superpowers of Santa. Where Jonathan Edwards sees "Sinners in the Hands of an Angry God," atheists see victims in the clutches of a maniacal one. What no one disputes is that it is fearsome to be on his bad side, no matter how the church nursery is painted. According to Dawkins, "The legend of the animals going into the ark two by two is charming, but the moral of the story of Noah is appalling. God took a dim view of humans, so he (with the exception of one family) drowned the lot of them including children and also, for good measure, the rest of the (presumably blameless) animals as well."[11] That is just the tip of his iciness, says Barker:

> We hear a lot of "God is love" sermons from the pulpit, but even a cursory glance at the Bible reveals that God kills a lot of people. He drowned the entire population of the planet, saving one family. He sent a plague to kill all the first-born children in Egypt, human and animal. He rained fire and brimstone on Sodom, killing everyone—boys, girls, babies, pregnant women, animals. He sent his Israelite warriors to destroy the neighboring pagan tribes—men, women and children.[12]

On the other hand, perhaps it is just as unfortunate to be one of the chosen on his good side. Citing the prohibitions on idolatry in Israelite law and the accompanying punishment by stoning, Harris writes, "The above passage is as canonical as any in the Bible, and it is only by ignoring such barbarisms that the Good Book can be reconciled with life in the modern world."[13] In other words, today such a judge would be thrown out of our courts. The only places he might find a job, thinks the atheist, are regions where age-old quarrels of rival gods have trickled down into everlasting war between adherents. Michel Onfray explains: "Thirty centuries, from the earliest texts of the Old Testament to the present day, teach us that the assertion of one God, violent, jealous, quarrelsome, intolerant, and bellicose, has generated more hate, bloodshed, deaths, and brutality than it has peace."[14] Atheists want reconciliation between people, and that necessitates divorce from the God whose punishments send us trembling into the old battle formations.

Unholy Cross: God as Pardoner

So the atheist asks God to lighten up, maybe enroll in anger management seminars. At the very least, he should stop killing people;

perhaps he could soften the sentence or try to be more understanding. Maybe he could channel all that wrath into creative, rather than destructive, avenues. But God offers a better solution. What if God were to take all that wrath, every bit of it, and ingest it back into himself, so that it need never threaten us again? To be exact, it would not be ingested into but rather boomeranged back upon himself. Regardless, the wrath would no longer be ours to shoulder, but his. What would the atheist say to that? If it has anything to do with a cross, the atheist says, "Thanks, but no thanks." There are six reasons the cross is unacceptable, even revolting, so that no real progress is made from the Old to New Testament.

First, Christ's redemption is said to be barbaric. If we did not applaud the animal sacrifices of the Old Testament, what will make us applaud the human sacrifice of the New? Both should make us shudder at humanity's primitive savagery. Harris explains, "The notion that Jesus Christ died for our sins and that his death constitutes a successful propitiation of a 'loving' God is a direct and undisguised inheritance of the superstitious bloodletting that has plagued bewildered people throughout history."[15]

Second, redemption is incoherent. In *The End of Christianity*, we discover that Bob Jones University–trained, Baptist-turned-atheist Ken Pulliam would have enjoyed time travel to further muddy up the christological heresy wars of the early Christian empire (as if that were even possible). For example, he asks why it is that only the Father needed to be propitiated when the three persons of the Godhead are allegedly equal. Moreover, did Jesus's atonement temporarily sever the unity of the Godhead, which is impossible? If not, then Jesus did not really die spiritually, and thus could not offer complete atonement. In the end, Pulliam concludes that the redemption story is incoherent.

Third, redemption is impossible. How can someone else take your sins upon himself? Impossible, says Christopher Hitchens: "We cannot, like fear-ridden peasants of antiquity, hope to load all our crimes onto a goat and then drive the hapless animal into the desert."[16] Pulliam remarks that "it is logically impossible to punish an innocent person."[17] Our evolved sense of justice forbids such a notion. Says Pulliam, "Punishment, according to the retributive theory of justice, is an appropriate response for one who is guilty of breaking the law. . . . [T]he guilty party and only the guilty party should be punished."[18]

Fourth, redemption is unnecessary. It sells a manufactured solution to a manufactured problem. On the one hand, if it can be assumed that original sin is a myth, then Dawkins is free to say, "So, in order to impress himself, Jesus had himself tortured and executed, in vicarious punishment for a *symbolic* sin committed by a *non-existent* individual? As I said, barking mad, as well as viciously unpleasant."[19] On the other hand, the notion of contemporary sin is dismissed as a myth as well. As Barker puts it, "It does no good to say that Jesus died on the cross to pay for our sins. I don't have any sins, but if I did, I wouldn't want Jesus to die for my sins. I would say, 'No, thanks. I will take responsibility for my own actions.'"[20] So the whole show—ailment and remedy—is unnecessary.

Fifth, redemption is obnoxious. Dawkins calls it a "repellant doctrine."[21] Elsewhere, he claims that it is "almost as morally obnoxious as the story of Abraham setting out to barbecue Isaac, which it resembles."[22] Nietzsche exclaims, "Sacrifice for sin, and in its most obnoxious and barbarous form: sacrifice of the innocent for the sins of the guilty!"[23] Moreover, if it is an obnoxious doctrine in the pages of the holy book, it is likewise obnoxious on your doorstep or in a tract under your windshield wiper. Hitchens explains, "It can be stated as a truth that religion does not, and in the long run, cannot, be content with its own marvelous claims and sublime assurances. It *must* seek to interfere with the lives of nonbelievers, or heretics, or adherents of other faiths."[24] In other words, believers can never be content to do the one thing Hitchens asks: "that they in turn leave me alone."[25]

Sixth and lastly, redemption is immoral. Hitchens paints the picture:

> Ask yourself the question: how moral is the following? I am told of a human sacrifice that took place two thousand years ago, without my wishing it and in circumstances so ghastly that, had I been present and in possession of any influence, I would have been duty-bound to try and stop it. In consequence of this murder, my own manifold sins are forgiven me, and I may hope to enjoy everlasting life.[26]

Recall Hitchens's answer: "I can pay your debt. . . . But I cannot absolve you of your responsibilities. It would be immoral of me to offer, and immoral of you to accept."[27] According to atheist professor Elizabeth Anderson, such "vicarious redemption" is immoral because it violates personal culpability: "The practice of scapegoating contradicts the whole moral principle of personal responsibility. It also contradicts any moral idea of God."[28] According to Pulliam, it is immoral because it punishes the innocent: "Is it ever moral to inflict suffering on someone as punishment for something they did not do? Our moral intuitions tell us that it is not."[29] Above all, it is immoral because it is child abuse at its worst. Barker writes, "I do understand what love is, and that is one of the reasons I can never again be a Christian. Love is not self-denial. Love is not blood and suffering. Love is not murdering your son to appease your own vanity."[30]

On the Other Hand

So the atheist's position is clear: punishment is bad; thus, pardon is unnecessary. Actually, such a summation is simplistic. First, it cannot be said that the atheist is anti-punishment. Take even Bertrand Russell, outspoken as he was against moral culpability. As someone who lived during the Holocaust, Russell urged treatment, not punishment, for many of the convicted Nazis. Notice, however, the revealing parenthetical element:

> In Germany at the present day, there are, of course, many men among the Nazis who are plain criminals, but there must also be many who are more or less mad. Leaving the leaders out of account (I do not urge leniency toward them), the bulk of the German nation is much more likely to learn cooperation with the rest of the world if it is subjected to a kind but curative treatment than if it is regarded as an outcast among the nations.[31]

Notice that even in perhaps the friendliest British reaction to the Holocaust of its day, punishment is still prescribed for many Germans. When the Germans are divided into criminals and madmen, the criminals, especially the leaders, do not escape punishment. Some incitements to punishment are not so friendly. From Peter Atkins's venomous quip, "May you rot in hell,"[32] to Hitchens's threat that abusive religious teachers ought to be glad hell was a myth "and that they were not sent to rot there,"[33] we find the atheist is not above what he would consider righteous anger. Some actions ought to be punished. Indeed, according to Harris, perhaps some people ought to be punished, even killed, on account of the very beliefs they hold:

> Some propositions are so dangerous that it may even be ethical to kill people for believing them. This may seem an extraordinary claim, but it merely enunciates an ordinary fact about the world in which we live. Certain beliefs place their adherents beyond the reach of every peaceful means of persuasion, while inspiring them to commit acts of extraordinary violence against others. There is, in fact, no talking to some people. If they cannot be captured, and they often cannot, otherwise tolerant people may be justified in killing them in self-defense.[34]

Some atheists are so convinced of the need for punishment that one of God's faults is being too lenient. According to Emma

Goldman, we must deal punishment precisely because God does not:

> The burden of all song and praise, "unto the Highest" has been that God stands for justice and mercy. Yet injustice among men is ever on the increase; the outrages committed against the masses in this country alone [Russia] would seem enough to overflow the very heavens. But where are the gods to make an end to all these horrors, these wrongs, this inhumanity to man? No, not the gods, but MAN must rise in his mighty wrath.[35]

So if punishment is not immoral in certain cases when administered by humans, why is it immoral when from God? It seems that were these atheists there at the collapsing of the Red Sea back on Pharaoh's army, or at the parade around Jericho's wall, they would have lined the sites with bullhorns and protest signs. What is their problem with God's punishments? Clearly, the issue is not punishment itself, which seems to be necessary. Instead, the problems seem to be culpability and extent. Take the flood. We find two possible problems with it. Either the people were innocent victims of God's overkill, or else they were flawed victims of God's oversights in programming their sense of right and wrong. He either punishes the innocent or creates the guilty. Either way, any extent of the punishment is always necessarily disproportionate to the crime. In this way, it can be said that, whatever the actions of the accused, punishment from God is always immoral. Being the severest in depth (death penalty) and width (human race), the flood is utterly unconscionable.

Recall from the first chapter, however, that such an argument is and must remain a God-in-the-Dock (GITD) argument. You cannot say that God is immoral to punish them and then introduce the atheistic assumption that they were innocent or that God created them guilty. The Bible is clear. At creation, Adam and Eve were created sinless and free, while in Noah's day, "The LORD saw that the wickedness of man was great in the earth, and that every intention of the thoughts of his heart was only evil continually" (Gen. 6:5). It cannot be assumed that this was a mass of duped sheep following a handful of extraordinarily evil people; no, this was a mass of extraordinarily evil people. Of course, if they were innocently murdered or robotically guilty, such a judgment can be called into question. But neither option is open to the atheist who is challenging the morality of God. While the morality is on trial, the historicity must be assumed. The question cannot fairly be, "Was it moral of God to condemn people that probably were not all that bad?" The question can only be, "Was it moral of God to condemn a people so thoroughly evil, by their own design, that they had become incapable of good?" To such a hideously culpable people, was the extent of the punishment too severe? Recall that even to Russell, the culpability of the action determines the extent of the punishment. In no less than the fiercest biblical case of punishment—the flood—extraordinary wickedness seems to demand a proportionate extent of punishment.

If the extent of the punishment depends on culpability, and if culpability is assumed biblically, as it must logically be, then the biblical extent of divine punishment seems completely permissible. Then how can the atheist still maintain his argument against divine punishment? For example, how can Harris, who does not condemn and perhaps even condones the death penalty for certain beliefs, denounce a God for plaguing the infanticidal Egyptians or for sending armies to chase out the child-sacrificing Canaanites from the promised land? We humans can administer whatever punishments we feel appropriate for the action, but God cannot, even toward people for whom "every intention of the thoughts of his heart was only evil continually" (Gen. 6:5). The problem cannot be punishment, for many, if not most, atheists are not anti-punishment. The problem cannot be culpability or extent, for in questioning God's character, the atheist must assume the utter lows of human culpability as found in the Bible. What is the problem then? Once again, the problem behind God's punishment is not punishment but God.

Yet perhaps that conclusion is simplistic. Suppose the wickedness of Noah's day, the infanticide of Moses's day, and the child sacrifices of Joshua's day were precisely as the Bible describes. Would such people deserve punishment, even death? Aside from some plan B that includes a reduction of freedom, most atheists would agree that such people, if they were really that awful, would deserve something similar to what they got. So the problem is merely that God is the one administering the punishment, right? No, the problem is not merely God but who we become when God is in the picture. If the atheist could affirm the depths of wickedness in those whom God punished, the atheist's objections would likely disappear, *but he cannot*. The problem is not merely that God punished them but the insult that they needed punishing. On entering, God introduces more than punishment; he introduces majestic holiness, unbending standards. In short, he makes us look bad. Under God, we are no longer evolving splendors but spoiled children. So the problem is still God, but it is not merely him but what he turns us into.

It is in this sense of what it implies about humanity that the atheists denounce divine punishment. It is possible that God could be justified in such extensive punishment but only if humanity could ever have been that bad. God is the problem because he makes us the problem. If it were not for this amplification of our wickedness, atheists could even pardon God for pardoning us. Forgiving us is not a problem in itself. Besides the costliness of the sacrifice, the problem is what such a costly sacrifice implies about humanity. It should have been so easy, says Anderson: "If God is merciful and loving, why doesn't he forgive humanity for its sins straightaway, rather than demanding his own son? How could any loving father do that to his son?"[36] Taking such great pains to solve such an easy problem is insanity, says Dawkins: "I have described atonement, the central doctrine of Christianity, as vicious, sado-masochistic and repellent. We should also dismiss it as barking mad, but for its ubiquitous familiarity which has dulled our objectivity. If God wanted to forgive our sins, why not just forgive them, without having himself tortured and executed in payment?"[37]

"Which would give you more dignity?" asks Barker. "[L]earning you were released because you were pardoned by the good graces of the governor, or because you were found to be innocent of the crime?"[38] Obviously, pardon via innocence would, and so that is the type of pardon God should have offered. Grace by faith is too demeaning. After Barker became an atheist, Barker's father followed suit. He told a reporter, "I'm much happier now. To be free from superstition and fear and guilt and the sin complex . . . is a tremendous relief."[39] That could have easily been a quote from a newly born-again Christian. The difference is that the senior Barker was freed from his sins by something much less costly than a cross. Atheists praise such "forgiveness." What they protest is not pardon itself but what the enormity of the debt's cancellation says about our debt. The problem with pardon is the same as the problem with punishment. The problem is neither punishment nor pardon but the imposition that is God. God-sized punishments and pardons alike magnify our mistakes to sins and reduce us to sinners. The problem is not that God is a wrathful judge or a merciful judge; we want neither. Presented two options—to be treated fairly (punishment) or unfairly (pardon), we opt for a third, in the form of a prayer of admonition to God: "Judge not, that You be not judged" (cf. Matt. 7:1).

7

Hell and Heaven

Promises of immortal salvation or fear of eternal damnation are both illusory and harmful. They distract humans from present concerns, from self-actualization, and from rectifying social injustices.

—*Humanist Manifesto II*[1]

"Afterlives are fantasies," laugh the atheists. They are fairy tales and horror novels. Some are written by the most cloud-headed among us, others by the most dark-hearted. They are daydreams that escape and compromise reality. The deeper it delves into such fictions, the further religion banishes itself from credibility, says the atheist. Although such confident pronouncements abound, arguing from the absurdity of the afterlife gets it backward. Once you are able to confirm that there is no God, then afterlives naturally disappear, but if God's existence remains a good possibility, then so do afterlives. Simply ridiculing afterlives doesn't further the debate. A more legitimate way, however, is to argue not that hell and heaven are ridiculous but that they are immoral, and that therefore a good God said to employ them could not actually exist. Such is the atheist's argument presented in this chapter. Now, the atheist cannot challenge the morality of hell and heaven by simply assuming them to be blatant absurdities, a caricature that stacks the deck against their legitimacy. It is no real victory to prove harps, haloes, pitchforks, and red suits to be too silly to believe in. If hell or heaven is under attack, let it be the real thing.

But how real is the afterlife? Within Christianity, the celestial world is firmer than our earth's crust. The here and now is a fleeting shadow, while the hereafter is a fixed surety. Instead of the afterlife being the novel, this life is the novel. "The End" *in* the book really means "Ever After" *outside* the book. The curtain closes; the playwright walks onstage. The artist signs his name at the bottom right and resumes life. The afterlife is the real-life realm of the author; what *we* call real life is the author's daydream. "Imagine there's no heaven," sings John Lennon.[2] Peter Rabbit might as well wish for the nonexistence of Beatrix Potter. Atheists will continue to ridicule the afterlife in the same tone they would use toward an adult believer in the tooth fairy. What must be conceded to be fair is that, if God exists, such a dimension is no mere tack-on but a necessity. Indeed, it is not *a* mere necessity but *the* necessity, whereas our realm is something similar to God's science fiction.

So if God exists, we, not hell and heaven, are God's embellishments. Whatever might be the basic stuff of the universe, eternity is the basic stuff of reality. Let us not have any nonsense about hell and heaven being harmful distractions that keep us from real work in the real world. Such talk assumes the nonexistence of God and only freezes the discussion. If God exists, then (no matter what happens in a person's lifetime) eternity with God and eternity without God exhaust the basic possibilities of a person's existence. So, as it would be only prudent for atheists to at least seriously consider God's existence, they must also consider hell and heaven. What if the atheist's lifetime has been God's daydream, and at death, the character awakes to his author? In the rudeness of the dawn, will he prefer the light or the darkness?

Hell: What the Doctrine Means for God

What is most surprising to atheists, and even to Christians, about hell is who came up with the idea. It was Jesus. This is quite disappointing because, on the whole, Jesus is quite likable. Bertrand Russell expresses his disappointment:

> There is one very serious defect to my mind in Christ's moral character, and that is that He believed in hell. I do not myself feel that any person who is really profoundly humane can believe in everlasting punishment. Christ certainly as depicted in the Gospels did believe in everlasting punishment, and one does find repeatedly a vindictive fury against those people who would not listen to His preaching.[3]

Dan Barker agrees: "Probably the worst of all of Jesus's ideas is the teaching of hell."[4] The reason is that "[a]ny system of thought or any religion that contains such a threat of physical violence is morally bankrupt."[5] Christopher Hitchens notes the irony: "Not until the advent of the Prince of Peace do we hear of the ghastly idea of further punishing and torturing the dead."[6] Though eternity with and without God exhaust the possibilities, the choices can seem a bit extreme, as Hitchens interprets the evangelist's presentation: "With an unctuous smile they offer a redemption that is not theirs to bestow and, when questioned, put on the menacing scowl that says, 'Oh, so you reject our offer of paradise? Well, in that case we have quite another fate in store for you.' Such love! Such care!"[7] It can seem as surprising as a mousetrap: from cheese to snap in a second.

Thus, the doctrine of hell shows God to be cruel. Former evangelist Charles Templeton found it impossible to work for such a God: "How could a loving Heavenly Father create an endless Hell and, over the centuries, consign millions of people to it because they do not or cannot or will not accept certain religious beliefs? And, having done so, how could he torment them *forever*?"[8] George H. Smith goes even further: "And why would God create a place of torment in the first place, unless he derived some kind of pleasure or satisfaction from witnessing pain? Whether the Christian deity of fire and brimstone projects love or neurotic sadism on a cosmic scale, will be left to the conscience of the reader to decide."[9] Whether necessitated by his system or requested for his pleasure, the fires of hell seem to disfigure God so that his love is either marred beyond recognition or burned away altogether.

Hell: What the Doctrine Means for Us

Likewise, the doctrine of hell is said to be immoral because of what it means for us. The "hell" it creates for us falls into two categories based on two kinds of people. First, it is devastating to the gullible—namely, those who believe it. The doctrine destroys three crucial relationships for those who believe it.

The first relationship destroyed for the gullible is relationship with self. If only they could "imagine there's no hell," they could salvage their lives from psychological shipwreck. According to Richard Dawkins,

> "Sticks and stones may break my bones, but words can never hurt me." The adage is true as long as you don't really *believe* the words. But if your whole upbringing, and everything you have ever been told by parents, teachers and priests, has led you to believe, *really believe*, utterly and completely, that sinners burn in hell (or some other obnoxious article of doctrine such as that a woman is the

property of her husband), it is entirely plausible that words could have a more long-lasting and damaging effect than deeds.[10]

Barker pulls no punches: "How many children go to sleep at night afraid of hell?"[11]

The second relationship destroyed is relationship with God. If a forced marriage stifles love, what would the threat of abuse do? According to atheists, the doctrine bullies believers into fake love. In a letter from God to the theologian, Barker has God say, "And if I did create a hell, then it certainly would not be smart to advertise that fact. How would I know if people were claiming to love me for my own sake, or simply to avoid punishment?"[12]

The third relationship destroyed is relationship with other people. In Russell's words, "I must say that I think all this doctrine, that hell-fire is a punishment for sin, is a doctrine of cruelty. It is a doctrine that put cruelty into the world and gave the world generations of cruel torture."[13] Atheist philosopher Keith Parsons calls the doctrine "an eternal glorification of vindictiveness" and asks, "How can an institution claim to be the Light of the World if one of its central doctrines is, to all appearances, an expression of the deepest darkness in the human heart?"[14] Such cruelty can even be legitimized for eternity. Note Hitchens's paraphrase of church father Tertullian, "promising that one of the most intense pleasures of the afterlife would be endless contemplation of the tortures of the damned."[15]

Not only is the doctrine of hell devastating to the gullible, but it is also useful to the corrupt. What such a scary doctrine does to control believers has not gone unnoticed by atheists. Hitchens surmises, "Perhaps half aware that its unsupported arguments are not entirely persuasive, and perhaps uneasy about its own greedy accumulation of temporal power and wealth, religion has never ceased to proclaim the Apocalypse and the day of judgment."[16] According to Emma Goldman, "Consciously or unconsciously, most theists see in gods and devils, heaven and hell, reward and punishment, a whip to lash the people into obedience, meekness and contentment."[17]

Now the question is what to do with such a doctrine. The first long-awaited task, says the atheist, is to call it what it is. Perhaps Charles Darwin did it best: "I can hardly see how anyone ought to wish Christianity to be true; for if so the plain language of the text seems to show that the men who do not believe, and this would include my Father, Brother and almost all my best friends, will be everlastingly punished. And this is a damnable doctrine."[18] The second task is to finally and decisively throw it out. Parsons prescribes, "With respect to the doctrine of hell, two thousand years are far more than enough. The damage this horrific and contemptible fantasy has done cannot be estimated. . . . Cruel dogmas make cruel people."[19]

Heaven: What the Doctrine Means for God

It is here that the plot twists. Clearly, the atheist does not want to go to hell. What the atheist might not yet realize is that God does not want him to go to hell either. All the facts considered, it is illogical to see the Christian God as one who delights in sending people to hell. Such a portrait is a shameful misrepresentation. But neither is it logical to see God as one who is basically displeased with sending people to hell. "Basically displeased" speaks of a mildness the Bible does not know. To be fair to the Bible, the portrait must be a shocking one of panting, frenzied desperation. How so? What we know is that the Christian God was so intensely against sending the atheist to hell that he went to hell himself, like a fireman to the rescue. God did not merely send an underling to the cross; the sacrifice was God in flesh. "It makes no difference," says the atheist, "because I don't believe in that kind of thing." No, by challenging the morality of God, the atheist must be prepared to deal with the real thing. And the cross is the twist central to the real thing.

So the atheist is not merely critiquing hell. It might sound permissible to sue someone for cutting you with a knife, something terrible in itself, until it comes to light that he was a surgeon removing something that might have killed you. In critiquing hell, the atheist is really attacking the whole surgery as immoral. Half-court scrimmage was back home; now, on the road, you are facing the real opponent, and it is this: God went through hell so the atheist could choose to go to heaven. But, in keeping with the two basic options of real, "out there" existence, the atheist can always reject the offer. It is understandable why the atheist would reject hell, but why reject heaven?

The first reason to reject heaven is what it says about God. God becomes something worse than the new stepdad (perfect according to mom), when he starts trying to buy and play his way into the role of loving father. Having to admit a God into your life in the first place is bad enough, having to worship him is worse, but having to love him is unthinkable. The obligations become increasingly unbearable, according to Hitchens:

> Imagine . . . that you can picture an infinitely benign and all-powerful creator, who conceived of you, then made and shaped you, brought you into the world he had made for you, and now supervises and cares for you even while you sleep. Imagine, further, that if you obey the rules and commandments that he has lovingly prescribed, you will qualify for an eternity of bliss and repose. I do not say that I envy you this belief (because to me it seems like the wish for a horrible form of benevolent and unalterable dictatorship).[20]

Take note, furthermore, that your new stepdad promises to snap into something akin to Cinderella's wicked stepmother when his love is not returned. For Barker, the threat of hell cancels out any joy of heaven: "Speaking for myself, if the biblical heaven and hell exist, I would choose hell. Having to spend eternity pretending to worship a petty tyrant who tortures those who insult his authority would be more hellish than baking in eternal flames. There is no way such a bully can earn my admiration."[21]

Heaven: What the Doctrine Means for Us

According to atheists, heaven means two different things for two different kinds of people. The first kind of person is the truly good person, and to such a person, the flattering enticements of heaven backlash into an insult. Hitchens explains,

> The working assumption is that we should have no moral compass if we were not somehow in thrall to an unalterable and unchallengeable celestial dictatorship. What a repulsive idea! . . . [I]t constitutes a radical attack on the very concept of human self-respect. It does so by suggesting that one could not do a right action or avoid a wrong one, except for the hope of a divine reward or the fear of divine retribution.[22]

Our moral convictions should be strong enough to withstand needing such threats and rewards, says Barker: "If the only way you can be forced to be kind to others is by the threat of hell, that shows how little you think of yourself. If the only way you can be motivated to be kind to others is by the promise of heaven, that shows how little you think of others."[23]

Yet a second kind of person is far from insulted by heaven. Instead, religion addicts need it to function. Their moral convictions are so flimsy that heaven is needed to prop them up. David Hume contrasts the truly moral with the superstitiously moral:

> The moral obligation, in our apprehension, removes all pretension to religious merit; and the virtuous conduct is deemed no more than what we owe to society and to ourselves. In all this, a superstitious man minds nothing, which he has properly performed for the sake of

his deity, or which can peculiarly recommend him to the divine favor and protection. He considers not that the most genuine method of serving the divinity is by promoting the happiness of his creatures. He still looks out for some immediate service of the supreme Being, in order to allay those terrors, with which he is haunted.[24]

Superstition makes for groveling, smirking subjects, as Dawkins notes. To the question "If there is no God, why be good?" Dawkins retorts,

> Posed like that, the question sounds positively ignoble. When a religious person puts it to me in this way (and many of them do), my immediate temptation is to issue the following challenge: "Do you really mean to tell me the only reason you try to be good is to gain God's approval and reward, or to avoid his disapproval and punishment? That's not morality, that's just sucking up, apple-polishing, looking over your shoulder at the great surveillance camera in the sky, or the still small wiretap inside your head, monitoring your every move, even your every base thought."[25]

So what is the atheist's problem with heaven? Regarding God, heaven turns him into that much more of a tyrant, not content to monitor behavior, but now needing to win our love as well. Never could more be demanded. Regarding us, heaven insults good people while enabling bad people by promising rewards for superficial conformity. In short, the atheist would hate heaven because he, being a good person, could not stand living in the presence of a bad God.

On the Other Hand

Not that hell is all it is fired up to be. Barker advises fellow atheists, "If someone tells me I am going to hell, I say, 'Thank you! All the great people are in hell. Elizabeth Cady Stanton, Mark Twain, Johannes Brahms, George Gershwin, Albert Einstein, Bertrand Russell, Margaret Sanger. . . . I was afraid you were going to tell me to "go to heaven" and spend eternity with Jerry Falwell.'"[26] Apparently, atheists can imagine one place worse than hell. Mark Twain was more balanced: "Heaven for climate; hell for society."[27]

Besides simply being not as bad as heaven, are there any perks to hell? It seems the doctrine probably does help improve behavior. Russell notes, "Those who genuinely believe that 'sin' leads to eternal punishment might be expected to avoid it, and to some extent they do so, although not to so great an extent as might be expected."[28] According to Parsons, it helps improve behavior, not that that is necessarily a good thing:

> Not only will the threat of hell prompt you to become a Christian, it will lead you to be a *submissive* one. All the stuff about faith, hope, and charity aside, *obedience* has always been the prime Christian virtue. . . . "There is no other way to be happy in Jesus but to trust and obey," says the old hymn. Indeed, the threat of hell will motivate not just external obedience but internal self-control as well.[29]

Before his conversion to Christianity, former atheist Peter Hitchens stood chilled before a piece of fifteenth-century artwork by Rogier van der Weyden called *The Last Judgment*. He recounts, "I had simply no idea that an adult could be frightened, in broad daylight and after a good lunch, by such things." Why was it so terrifying? "I had absolutely no doubt that I was among the damned, if there were any damned."[30] Did such fear make any moral difference? Says Hitchens, "A year or so later I faced a private moral dilemma in which fear of doing an evil thing held me back from doing it, for which I remain immeasurably glad."[31]

Perhaps a lesser-noted perk is the dignity hell gives humans. Theologians have long held that the decision to create hell was the ultimate compliment to human freedom. Who could have imagined tears splashing down the cheeks of Omnipotence as he cries, "[Y]ou were not willing!" (Matt. 23:37). Though such a compliment seems to go unnoticed by atheists, Russell notes a lesser compliment paid by hell: "The whole of theology, in regard to hell no less than to heaven, takes it for granted that Man is what is of most importance in the Universe of created beings."[32]

Of course, neither its ability to deter nor its compliment to human importance is enough to outweigh hell's problems for the atheist. But is the concept behind hell itself a problem? To refute philosopher William Lane Craig's contention that God is necessary for morality, Elizabeth Anderson argues that the moral authority must lie within humanity, so that we have "the authority to make claims on others, to call upon people to heed our interests and concerns."[33] Anticipating objections, she asks, "What of someone who refuses to accept such accountability? Doesn't this possibility vindicate Craig's worry, that without some kind of higher authority external to humans, moral claims amount to nothing more than assertions of personal preference, backed up by power?"[34] Note her solution: "No. We deal with people who refuse accountability by restraining and deterring their objectionable behavior."[35] Deterring and then restraining is precisely what God does with those who refuse his accountability, and it is called hell. However, to the atheist, the concept of warning followed by quarantine makes good sense unless enforced by God on a divine scale. It is really the same kind of double standard that surfaced when I (Norman) was telling people about Jesus door-to-door and met an atheist named Don:

Norman: "Don, if you were to die tonight and stand before God, and God were to ask you, 'Why should I let you into my heaven?' what would you say?"

Don: "I'd say to God, 'Why *shouldn't* you let me into your heaven?'"

Norman: "Don, if we knocked on your door seeking to come into your house, and you said to us, 'Why should I let you into my house?' and we responded, 'Why *shouldn't* you let us in?' what would you say?"

Don: "I would tell you where to go."

Norman: "That's exactly what God is going to say to you!"[36]

It is completely permissible for me to keep God out of my life, but for some reason, he cannot keep me out of his.

So hell has its merits. The concept behind hell—deterring and restraining the objectionable behavior of those who refuse accountability—is necessary in itself. Moreover, the motivation hell provides to good behavior and the compliment it pays to human dignity both keep it from being something entirely hellish. At any rate, hell has more in its favor than heaven for the atheist, like a Saturday night party compared to a Sunday morning worship service. On the other hand, we have yet to find an atheist mention a single positive with regard to heaven. It is no exaggeration to glean from their writings that heaven seems the most hellish place imaginable.

Yet what does the atheist say about the concept behind heaven? Is paradise really so distasteful? Well, for one thing, a real paradise would have to be in the real world. As Michel Onfray notes, "Their glorification of a (fictional) beyond prevents full enjoyment of the (real) here below."[37] For another, a true paradise must be discoverable not above, nor beside, but within humanity, as the *Humanist Manifesto I* makes clear: "Man is at last becoming aware that he alone is responsible for the realization of the world of his dreams, that he has within himself the power for its achievement."[38] But above all, paradise must be free from the parasite of religion, says Russell:

> With our present industrial technique, we can, if we choose, provide a tolerable subsistence for everybody. We could also secure that the world's population should be stationary if we were not prevented by the political influence of churches which prefer war, pestilence, and famine to contraception. The knowledge exists by which universal happiness can be secured; the chief obstacle to its utilization for that purpose is the teaching of religion. Religion prevents our

children from having a rational education; religion prevents us from removing the fundamental causes of war; religion prevents us from teaching the ethic of scientific co-operation in place of the old fierce doctrines of sin and punishment. It is possible that mankind is on the threshold of a golden age; but, if so, it will be necessary to slay the dragon that guards the door, and this dragon is religion.[39]

Thus, with the skies cleared of all divinities, we are free to rise to royalty over our paradise. As Salman Rushdie advises the earth's "six billionth person" in his letter, "Imagine there's no heaven, my dear Six Billionth, and at once the sky's the limit."[40] Until God leaves, heaven becomes hell, and as long as God stays away, hell becomes much preferable. Once again, the problem is neither hell nor heaven but God.

8

Inconsistencies

Truth does not ask to be believed. It asks to be tested.
—Dan Barker, *Godless*[1]

It is our sincere hope that we have so accurately represented the atheist thus far that he might be able to say, "Yes, that is what I believe." After all, we have tried to let the atheists speak for themselves. Here, where the discussion transitions into scrutiny, we take great reassurance in knowing atheists to be lovers of the rational. It is somewhat difficult to appreciate those who dismiss these sorts of questions as irrelevant. On the other hand, we admire those who extend the invitation to dialogue, those who recognize the importance of the questions. Atheists and Christians share the same playing field, as Sam Harris puts so well: "So let us be honest with ourselves: in the fullness of time, one side is really going to win this argument, and the other side is really going to lose."[2] What this levelness presupposes is that there exist shared rules that, when violated by either side, need to be reiterated. In this sort of dialogue, of course, the rules are those of rationality. We wish to crystallize our findings thus far by exposing two logical inconsistencies within atheism as it has presented itself.

Inconsistency 1: The Problem of Moral Evil versus the Problem of Divine Intervention

Recall the initial argument against the existence of God presented by the atheist. The atheist thinks God ought to fix the problem of moral evil. However, the atheist also values human autonomy, a value that helps us understand why the atheist rejects any interventions into the problem of moral evil that would threaten that autonomy. Thus, he ends up calling for freedom from submission and favor, death and faith, guilt and rules, punishment and pardon, hell and heaven. Recall the three categories of possible ways God could fix the problem of moral evil:

A ("All")—Forcible prevention of all moral evil

B ("Bad")—Forcible intervention into the most egregious cases of evil

C ("Conscience")—Voluntary intervention at the mental/spiritual level

From their writings, we learn that when the atheists say God should fix the problem of moral evil, they are suggesting A- or B-level interventions, both of which limit human freedom considerably. Yet in calling for freedom from the ten interventions, they rebuke God for merely C-level interventions. Astonishingly, they reject C-level interventions as too smothering, yet because God does not impose A- or B-level interventions, they charge him with neglect.

The contradiction is more pronounced than merely requesting help and then demanding freedom. As we have already mentioned, the ten interventions from which the atheist desires freedom are precisely the means by which the Christian God fixes the problem of moral evil. In this section, we will make the connection unmistakable; that is, the interventions being rejected do, in fact, help to fix the problem of moral evil. Furthermore, we will read from atheists themselves that such methods are effective in fixing the problem of moral evil. The only reason they might not seem effective enough, in the eyes of atheists, is that they are uncompromising in leaving freedom intact, something the freethinker should appreciate. In short, we will find that the atheist demands God fix the problem of moral evil while at the same time demanding freedom from the very methods God would use to fix it. Before proceeding, however, note once again that these are God-in-the-Dock (GITD) arguments. It might be tempting to deride the kind of morality produced by the following methods as, for example, too compliant or prostrate. Such valuations are beside the point, for the morality of the Christian system as a whole is under attack. God's existence, which is part of the system being attacked, makes such a worshipful morality not a vice but a virtue simply because there is, in fact, a Being worth worshiping.

Submission

First, the posture of submission so ridiculed by atheists yet so beloved to God is one of the very means by which God fixes the problem of moral evil. Humility before God not only pleases God but restores the sense of righteousness in people. Psalm 25:9 says of God, "He leads the humble in what is right, and teaches the humble his way." Proverbs 8:13a says, "The fear of the LORD is hatred of evil." James 4:7–8 connects submission with resistance to evil and purity of heart: "Submit yourselves therefore to God.

Resist the devil, and he will flee from you. Draw near to God, and he will draw near to you. Cleanse your hands, you sinners, and purify your hearts, you double-minded." Even Dan Barker links submission to obedience, though recoiling from obedience as if it were a loathsome thing:

> One of the most damaging ideas in the Bible is the concept of Lord and Master. The loftiest biblical principles are obedience, submission and faith, rather than reason, intelligence and human values. Worshippers become humble servants of a dictator, expected to kneel before this king, lord, master, god—giving adoring praise and taking orders.[3]

However, would not reason compel us to celebrate that which attempts to fix the problem of moral evil?

Favor

Where the atheist sees the arrogance of the saved, the Bible sees the gratitude of the once arrogant. Though it is definitely possible for beloved children to become spoiled, one of God's primary aims behind grace was moral transformation. And the Bible sets out at once to expose the shameful absurdity of any believer's arrogance. Romans 2:4 says, "Or do you presume on the riches of his kindness and forbearance and patience, not knowing that God's kindness is meant to lead you to repentance?" In 1 Corinthians 15:10, Paul made clear what motivated him: "But by the grace of God I am what I am, and his grace toward me was not in vain. On the contrary, I worked harder than any of them, though it was not I, but the grace of God that is with me." Even the sardonic Christopher Hitchens links appreciating God's special favor with furthering God's work in the world:

> Religion teaches people to be extremely self-centered and conceited. It assures them that god cares for them individually, and it claims

that the cosmos was created with them specifically in mind. This explains the supercilious expression on the faces of those who practice religion ostentatiously: pray excuse my modesty and humility but I happen to be busy on an errand from God.[4]

Jesus too deflated religious errands that were calculated to bring attention to oneself (Matt. 6:1). Yet Jesus was against neither favor from God nor errands for God. On the contrary, Jesus joined the two. It is when he calls his followers "light of the world" that he then commissions them to "let your light shine before others," not to be glorified, but "so that they may see your good works and give glory to your Father who is in heaven" (Matt. 5:14, 16).

Death

Was it really immoral of a reluctant God to permit death into his once-perfect world? Genesis 3:22–23a imagines what might have happened if he had not: "Then the Lord God said, 'Behold, the man has become like one of us in knowing good and evil. Now, lest he reach out his hand and take also of the tree of life and eat, and live forever—' therefore the Lord God sent him out from the garden of Eden." "How vengeful!" it might be exclaimed. On the contrary, how merciful: that is, if God cares about morality. Death was God's way of limiting the evil that had broken out. C. S. Lewis admits, "Perhaps my bad temper or my jealousy are gradually getting worse—so gradually that the increase in seventy years will not be very noticeable. But it might be absolute hell in a million years: in fact, if Christianity is true, Hell is the precisely correct technical term for what it would be."[5] The inevitability of death has a sobering effect on one's choices, as Hebrews 9:27 implies: "[J]ust as it is appointed for man to die once, and after that comes judgment." It certainly effected a repentance in the thief on the cross who went from mocking Jesus to correcting his fellow thief, as Luke 23:40–41 records: "Do you not fear God, since you are under the same sentence of condemnation? And we indeed justly, for we are receiving the due reward of our deeds; but this man has done nothing wrong."

Even atheists recognize the possibility that serious concern about one's death can effect a profound change in how one lives. Hitchens writes, "We are reconciled to living only once, except through our children, for whom we are perfectly happy to notice that we must make way and room. We speculate that it is at least possible that, once people accepted the fact of their short and struggling lives, they might behave better toward each other and not worse."[6] In fact, immortality would encourage lazy living, something that death's reality helps correct, says Barker: "We atheists believe in life *before* death. . . . What matters is that we are alive now. These living, breathing, hurting, singing, laughing bodies are *worth* something, for their own sake. Since there is no life after death . . . we have to make the most of it now, before it is too late."[7] In other words, death's surety helps to fix the problem of moral evil.

Faith

As hideous as faith is said to be, it is doubtful that its role in remedying the problem of moral evil will soften the atheist much. Yet the atheist cannot fairly deny at least that positive characteristic. Hebrews 11 lists faithful ancients who, precisely because of their faith, performed acts of sacrifice (v. 4), obedience (v. 8), rescue (v. 23), and justice (v. 33). James 2:18b connects faith to good works for the Christian: "I will show you my faith by my works." Though disapprovingly, Michel Onfray notes how inextricably faith in God is tied to obedience to God's moral instruction: "It all began with that ancient lesson from Genesis: man is forbidden to seek awareness; he should be content to believe and obey. He must choose faith over knowledge, suppress all interest in science, and instead prize submission and obedience."[8] Though "great faith" can be synonymous with terrorist hijackings, it should be recalled that, biblically, those with the greatest faith are those with the most love (James 2:14–17; 1 John 3:23).

Guilt

Just as the imperiled body needs pain to wake it up to danger, the culpable person needs guilt. Hitchens makes this clear:

> If I was suspected of raping a child, or torturing a child, or infecting a child with venereal disease, or selling a child into sexual or any other kind of slavery, I might consider committing suicide whether I was guilty or not. If I had actually committed the offense, I would welcome death in any form that it might take. This revulsion is innate in any healthy person, and does not need to be taught.[9]

But why is something as unpleasant as innate revulsion said to be healthy? It cannot be good for its own sake. As Barker asks, "What worse psychological damage could be done to children than to tell them that they basically are no good? What does this do to self-image?"[10] Rather, this innate revulsion must be healthy because of something it accomplishes, but what? For one thing, acute guilt can prevent the guilty one from doing the action again. For another thing, it might compel him to do whatever he can do to make things right for those he hurt. Moreover, if the revulsion had been strong enough, it might have prevented the offense from taking place in the first place.

In other words, guilt helps remedy the problem of moral evil. After repentance comes righteousness. This concept was foundational to Jesus's mission. He said in Mark 2:17, "Those who are well have no need of a physician, but those who are sick. I came not to call the righteous, but sinners." In other words, only those who recognize their sickness are able to be healed. Jesus could do nothing for the sins of smug saints, as his rebuke in John 9:41

makes clear: "If you were blind, you would have no guilt; but now that you say, 'We see,' your guilt remains." Adulterer and murderer King David experienced the transformative power of guilt, as he explains in Psalm 32:3, 5: "[W]hen I kept silent, my bones wasted away through my groaning all day long. . . . I acknowledged my sin to you, and I did not cover my iniquity; I said, 'I will confess my transgressions to the LORD,' and you forgave the iniquity of my sin." If you imagine how mangled a body would be without the sense of pain, then you get a picture of a soul without a sense of guilt.

Rules

It is almost laughable that a paragraph would be needed to show that having rules from God aids us in being more moral, but it is definitely conceivable that certain atheists might be cantankerous enough to dissent. Remember, however, because these are GITD arguments, the challenger must not insert unchristian assumptions, but must take everything into consideration as is. Thus, biblical sins such as idolatry, blasphemy, and such cannot be dismissed as victimless and thus illusory crimes. Even without this stipulation, however, atheists admit that at least some of the biblical rules help fix the problem of moral evil, even though these rules are supposedly superfluous to the truly good people who already knew them. Harris admits, "It is true, of course, that Jesus said some profound things about love and charity and forgiveness. The Golden Rule really is a wonderful moral precept."[11] God's rules do help fix the problem of moral evil, whether against God or humans.

According to Deuteronomy 6:24–25, the aim of the law of Moses was to help fix the problem of moral evil: "And the LORD commanded us to do all these statutes, to fear the LORD our God, for our good always, that he might preserve us alive, as we are this day. And it will be righteousness for us, if we are careful to do all this commandment before the LORD our God, as he has commanded us." In fact, it seems the primary reason the commandments were so treasured is that they helped to fix the problem of moral evil. Psalm 119:11 says, "I have stored up your word in my heart, that I might not sin against you." Psalm 119:127–28 says, "Therefore I love your commandments above gold, above fine gold. Therefore I consider all your precepts to be right; I hate every false way." Psalm 119:172 says, "My tongue will sing of your word, for all your commandments are right."

Punishment

It might seem difficult to make a case that the judgments in the Bible help fix the problem of moral evil. After all, the problem passages often seem to record a punishment that goes one step further than the refiner's fire so that the punished ends up burned to a crisp. However, there are two ways those sorts of judgments helped fix the problem of moral evil. First, they served as a future warning. "And he called out, 'Yet forty days, and Ninevah shall be overthrown!' And the people of Ninevah believed God. They called for a fast and put on sackcloth, from the greatest of them to the least of them" (Jonah 3:4–5). Christians are not exempt from such warnings, as in Colossians 3:5–7: "Put to death therefore what is earthly in you: sexual immorality, impurity, passion, evil desire, and covetousness, which is idolatry. On account of these the wrath of God is coming. In these you too once walked, when you were living in them."

The second way the punishments in the Bible help fix the problem of moral evil is as a past example. Referring to the Israelites who dropped dead in the wilderness on the way to the promised land, Paul writes in 1 Corinthians 10:6, "Now these things took place as examples for us, that we might not desire evil as they did." Likewise, recalling a plague in which twenty-three thousand people died, Paul in 1 Corinthians 10:11 says, "Now these things happened to them as an example, but they were written down for our instruction." Verse 12 applies all this: "Therefore let anyone who thinks that he stands take heed lest he fall." Those who take such judgments seriously can be expected to try to live more morally. Though he invalidly divorces the ethical endeavor from the motivation to please God, Barker basically agrees: "People who believe they are living under the thumb of such a vain and petty lord are not guided by ethics; they are guided by fear. The bible turns out to be not a moral code, but a whip."[12] Barker calls it a whip, but after all, whips get results, which is precisely what the problem-of-evil atheists are asking God for. In fact, one might even argue that at last God is almost reaching B-level interventions.

Pardon

Can the cross really help fix the problem of moral evil? Does it not merely let us off the hook, fueling our irresponsibility while God takes responsibility for the wickedest crime in history? In other words, does it not make both God and humanity more immoral? Such questions forget the nature of love. First of all, Jesus was no mere servant, the unfortunate victim of a master's thoughtless planning. *Immanuel* means "God with us." "In the beginning was the Word, and the Word was with God, and the Word was God" (John 1:1). That was God himself on the cross. Second, love begets love. According to Hitchens, "Once again we have a father demonstrating love by subjecting a son to death by torture, but this time the father is not trying to impress god. He *is* god, and he is trying to impress humans."[13] And does it work? For those who truly reflect on what happened there, the only two appropriate responses happen to be the only responses you would say to a marriage proposal. Recklessly firing out a "Sure, sounds good. Let me get back to my video game" is not an option. Such embarrassingly extravagant love can only be rejected or requited. Those who love him back will live the rest of their lives in gratitude.

So yes, being forgiven of one's sins through such conspicuous love encourages righteousness. After all, Jesus said in John 14:15, "If you love me, you will keep my commandments." Paul summarizes the process in Ephesians 2:8–10: "For by grace you have been saved through faith. And this is not your own doing; it is the gift of God, not a result of works, so that no one may boast. For we are his workmanship, created in Christ Jesus for good works, which God prepared beforehand, that we should walk in them." That is, we are saved not just from our sins but from our sinfulness, so that we can finally and truly do good works. To feel the burden of one's sinfulness drop is such glorious freedom, as Barker's atheist father mentions but misapprehends: "I'm much happier now. To be free from superstition and fear and guilt and the sin complex, to be able to think freely and objectively, is a tremendous relief."[14]

Hell

We turn now to two methods God uses that, much like punishment, work on the conscience before they actually take place. In that sense, they are C-level interventions in this life. Does the anticipation of hell's reality help fix the problem of moral evil? Yes, says atheist Keith Parsons. Recall his words:

> Not only will the threat of hell prompt you to become a Christian, it will lead you to be a *submissive* one. All the stuff about faith, hope, and charity aside, *obedience* has always been the prime Christian virtue. . . . "There is no other way to be happy in Jesus but to trust and obey," says the old hymn. Indeed, the threat of hell will motivate not just external obedience but internal self-control as well.[15]

The Bible agrees. A passage that sobers any serious-minded Christian is Matthew 25:41–43, 45b:

Then he will say to those on his left, "Depart from me, you cursed, into the eternal fire prepared for the devil and his angels. For I was hungry and you gave me no food, I was thirsty and you gave me no drink, I was a stranger and you did not welcome me, naked and you did not clothe me, sick and in prison and you did not visit me. . . . As you did not do it to one of the least of these, you did not do it to me."

Does that passage motivate loving action? Of course! As easy as it is to brand oneself "a loving person" without actually doing anything for anybody, it is a good thing for the world that there are some authoritative reinforcements. Likewise, Galatians 5:20–21 lists "idolatry, sorcery, enmity, strife, jealousy, fits of anger, rivalries, dissensions, divisions, envy, drunkenness, orgies, and things like these," and adds, "I warn you, as I warned you before, that those who do such things will not inherit the kingdom of God."

Heaven

There is no effort at all in explaining how the promise of heaven can motivate good behavior. After all, says Jesus in Matthew 7:21, "Not everyone who says to me, 'Lord, Lord,' will enter the kingdom of heaven, but the one who does the will of my Father who is in heaven." And even though Richard Dawkins calls it "just sucking up, apple-polishing, looking over your shoulder at the great surveillance camera in the sky,"[16] it still effects moral change. Of course, according to the atheists, it is not the right kind of change, but it is change in the right direction nonetheless. But could this futuristic reward motivate the "right" kind of change?

Recall what heaven is. The Bible hints with imagery, but what we know for sure is that heaven is where God is. As Revelation 21:3b envisions, "Behold, the dwelling place of God is with man. He will dwell with them, and they will be his people, and God himself will be with them as their God." Who would not want to sign up? Unfortunately, many would willfully decline, and not just atheists. After all, when Jesus came the first time, "the Word became flesh and dwelt among us, and we have seen his glory" (John 1:14a), and yet, "He came to his own, and his own people did not receive him" (John 1:11). Why? "[T]his is the judgment: the light has come into the world, and people loved the darkness rather than the light because their works were evil" (John 3:19). Biblically, the primary, if not the only, reason people reject heaven is that they love evil more than they love God. The treasure of heaven is simply not treasured by many people because heaven's treasure is not a mansion but a Person. And only "the pure in heart . . . shall see God" (Matt. 5:8). C. S. Lewis explains,

> We are afraid that heaven is a bribe, and that if we make it our goal we shall no longer be disinterested. It is not so. Heaven offers nothing that a mercenary soul can desire. It is safe to tell the pure in heart that they shall see God, for only the pure in heart want to. There are rewards that do not sully motivations. A man's love for a woman is not mercenary because he wants to marry her, nor his love for poetry mercenary because he wants to read it, nor his love of exercise less disinterested because he wants to run and leap and walk. Love, by definition, seeks to enjoy its object.[17]

That is why heaven not only encourages righteousness but also satisfies the righteous.

As we have seen, the atheist claims that God is not perfectly good or all-powerful because he has not fixed the problem of moral evil. Yet the atheist desires freedom from the very tools God naturally uses to fix the problem of moral evil, even charging God to be immoral for employing them. To fix the problem of moral evil and yet keep free will intact, God employs C-level interventions, which the atheist detests because they threaten his autonomy. Yet the same atheist thinks it immoral that God does not employ A- or B-level interventions to fix the problem of moral evil. What we have here is a self-refuting position. Put simply, the atheist is complaining that "God should fix the problem, but he shouldn't touch anything." "He should take away our freedom but in such a way that he doesn't take away an ounce of freedom." "He's never around; what's more, he never leaves us alone!"

Inconsistency 2: Divine Intervention versus Societal Intervention

The first inconsistency lies in calling God too negligent for not fixing the problem of moral evil and then calling his interventions that go to fix moral evil too smothering. Thus, the atheist overrules the argument based on moral evil by arguing against the morality of divine interventions. In a second inconsistency, the atheist seems to reverse stances on the immorality of the divine interventions. Whereas he argues scathingly against the morality of these interventions at the divine level, somehow these interventions turn out not to be problematic at the societal level. In this section, we will review the atheist's aversion to each of the divine interventions before summarizing the reversal of each attack when applied to the societal level.

Submission and Favor

It would seem that if there were a God, he could view creatures in two possible ways. First, all creatures would start out as servants, doing the kinds of things they were created to do. It seems that the Creator-creature relationship demands this sort of subordination by definition. Second, however, it is conceivable that a God could elevate a servant to a higher rank of some kind, perhaps even up to being a sharer in some qualities of divinity, such as freedom. But at root, this elevated creature will, or at least ought to, always be a servant, though an elevated one. If the atheist decries the role of submissive servant as too demeaning, it would seem he would logically favor the only other option, the divine favor—freedom, image of God, redemption—offered humanity by the Christian God. But the atheist wants neither of these possibilities, exclusive as they are. The atheist cannot denounce submission without embracing favor, and he cannot denounce favor without embracing submission. Yet he attempts both.

Death and Faith

Then there is the confusion about the first chapters of Genesis. While theologians dispute the meaning of the word *day*, atheists contemplate a more pragmatic question: Is the garden of Eden a paradise or a prison? That is, would I want to enjoy or escape? Perhaps the atheist even dismisses the question as absurd: "You don't expect me to believe that fairy tale!" However, recall that these are GITD arguments; the atheist cannot challenge the morality of the system God set up by caricaturing the system as a fairy tale. So back to the garden of Eden we go. The atheist says that it is immoral of God to permit the entrance of death into the world. According to Genesis, yes, it was immoral, but not of God. He had set up a system of reliance on him, called faith. The first humans chose to unchain themselves from the Source of life. Death was warned by God, yes, but it is only logical that death would have inevitably followed the transgression even without the decree. True, death and faith were the only two options presented in the garden of Eden, but would not the two options—binding or unbinding yourself from the Source of life—be the only two conceivable options in dealing with God regardless?

Yet the atheist rejects both death from God and faith in God as despicably immoral. When it is suggested that the two are exclusive and the atheist must choose one or the other, suppose the atheist counters that the whole setup itself is immoral, a case of "choose your poison." In response, first, if God exists, both options do seem to be the only logical alternatives, regardless of how they taste. Second, however, recall what we learned in chapter 4, that the atheist has no real difficulties with death or faith, provided God is not involved. "Objection!" protests the atheist, for the problem he has is not with death as such but with death by God's hand. There is a moral difference between someone dying by smallpox and by murder, after all. But is God really actively administering death? Check the story. There is no divine execution; Adam and Eve live. They simply lose access to immortality, something that logically could only be sustained by the relationship they severed. If the atheist denounces the one alternative, he ought to embrace its opposite. Yet both are somehow simultaneously immoral.

Guilt and Rules

As we saw in chapter 5, even atheists believe guilt is necessary where there is culpability. Of course, atheists dispute where to draw the line, but when someone has crossed that line, guilt is recognized as only healthy. Yet God is somehow immoral for simply making us *feel* guilty, even within a system in which culpability is shockingly real. How dare he be so petty and cruel! On the other hand, his proposed path to sidestepping guilt is equally immoral, for as a rule, his prescriptions are always flawed. Any rules we would not obey are, of course, not worth obeying. Any rules we would obey anyway he plagiarized. (Plagiarized from what? As if the infinitely and necessarily rational God would need to copy tiny bipedal sages! If there really are timeless, discoverable moral truths, where do you think they came from?) Whatever the case, the atheist desires to ignore the rules and yet be counted blameless. In the end, the atheist rejects both of the logical possibilities in dealing with a moral God—obeying the rules and reaping the guilt—as immoral.

Punishment and Pardon

From their writings, it seems clear that many atheists read through the Bible like proofreaders, looking for errors. A disproportionate number of checkmarks seem to always cluster toward the front, in the history passages of the Old Testament. The flood, the plagues, the conquest of Canaan—with guilt itself as immoral, the next step of actual punishment is unspeakable. It matters not that every inclination of man's heart "was only evil continually" (Gen. 6:5b). God is still the bad guy of the story. This tells us that no matter how evil anyone gets, it is never moral for God to punish. Never mind the many atheists who advocate retribution against the monsters among us, especially since September 11, 2001. If judgment is necessary in some cases, would not an all-just God be permitted, even compelled, to administer punishment in some cases? For some reason, he is not.

So a just God cannot carry out justice. He cannot treat people fairly. Can he, therefore, treat them unfairly? No, because that violates his nature. But what if God were to treat people unfairly in a way that is still fair to his perfect justice? Romans 3:26 tells us that the purpose of the cross was to demonstrate "[God's] righteousness at the present time, so that he might be just and the justifier of the one who has faith in Jesus." The voluntary cross is the means by which God justifies the guilty and yet remains just. Yet the red blood of such passages mingles with the red pen of the atheist. In the end, a just God cannot judge lest he be judged, and a merciful God can show no mercy.

Hell and Heaven

First of all, it must be reiterated that the afterlife is not an afterthought. Since God's existence is part of the Christian system being attacked, the atheist cannot caricature the afterlife as if God did not exist. If God exists, this life is as dependent on the next as a novel is dependent on its author's mind. Heaven and hell are not merely tacked on to this life like an epilogue. Eternity with and without God are the two basic, mutually exclusive types of reality; this life is merely our time to choose between them. Thus we can see how foolish it is to say, "It is immoral of God to send us to hell or to bring us to heaven," as if the best thing is to be left alone in the so-called real world. Out there is the real world, and with or without God seem to be fairly straightforward, inevitable options. Yet the atheist wants neither hell nor its far-more-hellish opposite.

Reversal

And yet, are these interventions truly as immoral as all that? As decisively as the atheist denounces the divine interventions as immoral, one would think that the interventions themselves must be truly despicable. Yet when the atheist considers the concept behind these interventions played out in a *societal* context, we find the atheist excusing them as not immoral in the least. Submission? Recall with Dawkins that were we to be contacted by highly evolved extraterrestrials, "A pardonable reaction would be something akin to worship."[18] Favor? Recall with Bertrand Russell that "[f]or in all things it is well to exalt the dignity of man."[19] Death? Recall with Barker that "[t]he scarcity and brevity of life is what enlarges its value. . . . If life is eternal, then life is cheap."[20] Faith? Recall with Russell that "[i]n this lies man's true freedom: in determination to worship only the God created by our own love of the good, to respect only the heaven which inspires the insight of our best moments."[21] Guilt? Recall Hitchens's candor that "[i]f I was suspected of raping a child, or torturing a child, or infecting a child with venereal disease, or selling a child into sexual or any other kind of slavery, I might consider committing suicide whether I was guilty or not. . . . This revulsion is innate in any healthy person."[22]

Rules? Recall with Russell that "[w]hat we have to do positively is to ask ourselves what moral rules are most likely to promote human happiness."[23] Punishment? Recall with Harris that "[s]ome propositions are so dangerous that it may even be ethical to kill people for believing them."[24] Pardon? Recall with Dawkins that there is an entirely appropriate type of pardon God could learn from humanity: "If God wanted to forgive our sins, why not just forgive them, without having himself tortured and executed in payment."[25] Hell? Recall with Elizabeth Anderson that in any healthy society, "We deal with people who refuse accountability by restraining and deterring their objectionable behavior."[26] Heaven? Sounds great! Recall with Russell that "[t]he knowledge exists by which universal happiness can be secured."[27] However, as is the case with all ten of these so-called problems, "The chief obstacle to its utilization for that purpose is the teaching of religion."[28] Like an enormous mountain in the path of an expanding railroad, God is in the way. The problem is decidedly *not* the interventions themselves; the problem seems to be not merely aggravated but basically caused by the fact that *God* proposes them. These ten things are fine in themselves. The problem is the God who turns heaven into hell and whose absence makes hell seem almost heavenly.

As we have seen, the atheist is not at all shy insisting on what he wants, and yet isn't quite sure what he wants after all. He wants neither a thing nor its opposite, even though together they present the only possible alternatives. Moreover, the things he calls immoral he then calls moral. We apologize in advance for jerking this out of context, but Dawkins's question seems appropriate: "Why don't they notice those glaring contradictions?"[29] Yet there is a way to sidestep each inconsistency—namely, to simply be rid of God. Unfortunately, it is precisely in trying to sidestep God that the atheist entangles himself in these inconsistencies in the first place.

9

Responses and Objections

One thought kept rising to the surface, as if spoken from somewhere else: "Something is wrong." I couldn't figure it out. I couldn't really articulate the questions properly, but a voice in my mind kept saying, "Something is wrong. Admit it."

—Dan Barker, *Godless*[1]

So where do we go from here? We have discovered two logical inconsistencies in atheistic arguments. As we have seen in two arguments, no sooner does the atheist level his accusation against the Christian God than he invalidates the argument. In the first case, though initially indicting God for not fixing the problem of moral evil, the atheist then indicts God for his attempts to fix it. Somehow, God is immoral for being too permissive and then immoral for being too inhibiting. Why are his interventions seen as too inhibiting? Because they threaten something the atheist greatly values—namely, human autonomy. Thus, the appeal to the problem of moral evil is overturned by appeal to the problem of divine intervention. Then we find a second inconsistency, this one overturning their appeal to the problem of divine intervention. Although denouncing as evil the interventions that God proposes in order to fix moral evil, the atheist then reverses himself by absolving those same types of interventions on a societal level. Apparently, the problem is not the interventions themselves so much as the one wielding them. Why is God condemned as immoral to propose these interventions when they are excused and even appreciated on a societal level?

Let us suggest a proper atheistic response for each of these two inconsistencies before considering some potential objections to these responses. First, what should be the proper response of the atheist to the first inconsistency, wherein the atheist overturns his appeal to the problem of moral evil by appealing to the problem of divine intervention? Well, when you have two opposing propositions, you must let loose of one of them to remain within rationality. The atheist presents two requests to God that cannot both be logically granted. Quite simply, God cannot fix the problem of moral evil without intervening to fix the problem of moral evil. Keep in mind that the atheist's contradiction, however, is even more absurd, for the atheist is asking God for something no less drastic than A- or B-level interventions and yet denouncing mere C-level interventions as too smothering. If you realize that you cannot hold both complaints without contradiction, then honesty demands that you simply let go of one of the complaints. On the one hand, the atheist can argue with the system of freedom the Christian God set up in the first place and ask, "Why doesn't God solve the problem of moral evil?" If so, he must drop his objections to God's C-level interventions, because, of course, those are God's solution to the problem of moral evil. On the other hand, the atheist can argue with the interventions God offers and ask, "Why does God have to intervene so much?" In so doing, however, he must drop the objection that God does not intervene because, of course, he does. So in light of the first inconsistency, the most natural and rational response would be to let go of either the argument indicting God for not fixing moral evil or the argument indicting God for intervening to fix it.

What would be a rational response to the second inconsistency? Recall that submission and favor, death and faith, guilt and rules, punishment and pardon, hell and heaven are all said to be immoral on the divine level, yet their counterparts on a societal level are vindicated. It would seem that if something is not immoral at the societal level, it should not be condemned at the divine level either. Where exactly do we find the immorality? If God is the subject and his interventions are the verb, suppose the atheist says that the subject *God* is the immorality. In other words, God is immoral because God is immoral. This would be circular reasoning. Suppose the atheist responds instead that the immorality lies in what God *does*. But the interventions have already been absolved at the societal level. Clearly, the atheist does not see the verb as immoral in itself. Thus, why indict God for something that is not immoral? Rationality demands consistency. It seems the natural and rational response would be to either condemn these interventions as immoral *in themselves*, or to concede that God is not, in fact, immoral in employing them.

Thus, we are proposing to the atheist a response for each of the two inconsistencies, responses that would, in fact, resolve the two inconsistencies. In short, they are:

1. Either drop the argument appealing to the problem of moral evil or drop the arguments claiming that God's interventions to fix the problem of moral evil are immoral.
2. Stop labeling as immoral those interventions that the Christian God proposes while simultaneously claiming that their counterparts on the societal level are not immoral.

Now let us consider some objections the atheist might advance to elude the responses that have been proposed. Objections 1–3 correspond to the first proposed response, while objections 4–5 correspond to the second.

Objection 1: I Maintain That God Should Fix Only the Worst Kinds of Moral Evil

What if, in relation to the argument appealing to the problem of moral evil, an atheist holds to only part of the argument as stated? The atheist could say something like, "Now, I never suggested that God should get rid of *all* instances of evil. But, if he's truly a good God, then *at the very least* he should have thwarted monsters like Hitler. I mean, if he really loves us, he should at least prevent child abuse." If the atheist softens the demands with regard to the problem of moral evil, can he then rationally hold both arguments at the same time (i.e., it is immoral of God to permit the worst cases of moral evil and likewise immoral of him to propose the interventions to fix moral evil)?

Response to Objection 1

It will be helpful to recall the three possible levels of intervention into the problem of moral evil presented earlier:

A ("All")—Forcible prevention of all moral evil

B ("Bad")—Forcible intervention into the most egregious cases of evil

C ("Conscience")—Voluntary intervention at the mental/spiritual level

This first objection basically asserts that asking God for merely B-level interventions does not cancel out the repudiation of divine interventions when they come. Recall that B-level interventions would still rob the human of a tremendous treasure of autonomy. If God were to prevent the worst types of evil, this would translate into either constitutional constraints on what humans were capable of or the miraculous thwarting of innumerable actions. Even softening his request for interventions from A to B level, the atheist is still asking for something miraculous and then demanding its removal.

Moreover, the atheist desiring B-level intervention who hopes to elude contradiction overlooks an important fact of logic. The following statements cannot both be true:

1. All moral problems should be fixed by God.
2. No moral problems should be fixed by God (even at the C-level).

Statement 1 represents A-level intervention, and statement 2 represents the atheist's demand for freedom from mere C-level interventions. Yet does the contradiction resolve itself when the first statement is reduced from A-level to B-level?

1. Some moral problems should be fixed by God.
2. No moral problems should be fixed by God (even at the C-level).

With statement 1 now as B level, it is a fact of logic that the two statements have become *direct* contradictions. Thus, the atheist who softens the problem of moral evil into demanding that God fix only the worst cases of evil does not elude contradiction at all.

Objection 2: I Maintain That Only Some of These Divine Interventions Are Immoral

The atheists we have consulted have attacked ten divine interventions that God would use to fix the problem of moral evil. What if an atheist holds only certain of these interventions to be immoral?

For example, of the ten interventions, what if an atheist holds numbers 1–5 to be immoral, but not numbers 6–10? Is the atheist still contradicting his accusation that God ought to fix the problem of moral evil?

Response to Objection 2

The reason there is a contradiction in the first place is that the atheists we have looked at want freedom from something that God would naturally use to remedy the problem of moral evil. Thus, if the atheist desires freedom from even one intervention that God would use to remedy the problem of moral evil, while at the same time judging God as immoral for not fixing the problem of moral evil, he is contradicting himself. It is inconsequential how many cries for freedom go forth; even one calls into question the seriousness of the atheist's complaint against moral evil.

It seems clear from the atheists' writings that these ten interventions are in fact things that the atheist desires freedom from. Of course, there is the possibility of an atheist holding one or more of the ten interventions as immoral and yet not actually desiring freedom from what he is rejecting. For example, it is possible to hold that God's method of redeeming sinners (the crucifixion of Christ) is immoral because it involves punishment of the innocent but not necessarily to desire freedom from redemption itself. It is possible that an atheist could want God to fix the problem of moral evil, object to his methods (i.e., the ten interventions), and yet not necessarily want freedom from them. Keep in mind the rarity of such an atheist, however; for not only must he *not* desire freedom from any of the ten interventions, but he must truly desire even more imposing interventions (A or B level) than those attributed to the Christian God (merely C level) if he is to hold that God ought to fix the problem of moral evil. If such an atheist exists, he is exempt from our critique. But thanks to atheists' commitment to human autonomy, their writings make it seem almost a prerequisite for them to desire at least some freedom from God. After all, even Christians sometimes desire freedom from some of God's interventions. Are Christians always pleased with his project of making them holy as he is holy? Countless sermons are preached to squirming Christians urging them to trust in his interventions, however it inhibits their autonomy. The difference between the Christian and the atheist is that in our reflective moments we Christians realize that such desires for freedom from God's interventions indicate *our* immorality, not God's.

Objection 3: Even If Not Immoral, God Could Have Done It a Better Way

This objection assumes that, in fact, it is a contradiction to say that God should intervene to fix the problem of moral evil and yet that his interventions are immoral because they threaten human autonomy. God is not necessarily inactive in the face of moral evil, and he is not necessarily inimical to human freedom. However, this objection contends rather that there is a *better* way God could have set things up, something more godlike. Perhaps we cannot call God immoral, but we could still argue that there is a better way God could have done it. We could imagine a better God.

Response to Objection 3

Regarding moral freedom and divine interventions, what are the logically possible ways God could have set things up better? There appear to be two ways. Perhaps, on the one hand, God could have intervened more so that the problem of moral evil would be less of a problem. Or, on the other hand, perhaps God could have given humanity even greater autonomy. Given the alleged problems with the way God set things up, these seem to be the two possible ways

God could have improved. Notice what happens, however, with each potential tweak. The more God intervenes into the problem of moral evil, the less potential autonomy humanity has. Conversely, the more autonomy humanity is granted, the fewer the interventions that are permitted. Such a trade is only logical. What we find here is nothing profound but is nonetheless something that should not be forgotten—namely, that freedom and intervention are on opposite ends of the seesaw. When one goes up, the other goes down. It would be absurd to propose that God be more forceful in fixing the problem of moral evil while at the same time proposing that he increase freedom. As C. S. Lewis says, "You may attribute miracles to him, but not nonsense."[2]

To put a picture above this caption, imagine that the atheist who advances this objection decides that a better God would give humanity more freedom (and thus less intervention). It would appear then that the Christian God, though not exactly immoral, is not a palatable God to that particular atheist. Rather, the atheist now finds himself before a new God, one that produces interventions less fatefully, and thus encourages a freedom less uptight. John Hick, for example, has proposed a divinely structured system of multiple lives that advance oneself, in the end, to moral and spiritual fulfillment without resorting to anything as drastic as a final judgment.[3] Or perhaps certain more modern renditions of Judaism, according to which God is far more concerned with everyday ethics than with afterlives, might be more amenable to the atheist.

So the atheist finds himself window-shopping for another religion, which is completely permissible but lies outside the scope of this work. The atheist then obligates himself to argue against the new God in order to retain his atheism, but this should prove difficult since he has just stumbled upon a God that eludes his critique. If he goes ahead and buys into the new religion, he is obviously no longer an atheist. If he does not, he still has to reckon with a Christianity that has yet to be disproved. Whatever the case, the atheist who values a moral humanity as well as a free humanity would have trouble finding a God more uncompromisingly committed to the same goals than the Christian God.

Objection 4: These Interventions Are Necessary on a Societal but Not Divine Level

Whereas on a societal level these types of interventions are necessary, they are unnecessary on the divine level. If God were really all-wise and all-powerful, he would not have to resort to such unnecessary methods to fix the problem of moral evil. It was never claimed that humanity was infinitely wise or powerful; thus, such interventions are not immoral on the societal level. But God should be able to come up with better ways to fix the problem of immorality that are not themselves immoral.

Response to Objection 4

Two assertions are being made here. First, these interventions *are* basically immoral, but necessary on a societal level. Second, since they are not necessary on the divine level, God is immoral to employ them. However, we assert that these interventions do follow naturally, even necessarily, from the very nature of the Christian God. As we shall see, perfectly moral interventions flow from the nature of a perfectly moral God.

According to the atheists we have consulted, it is immoral of God to permit moral evil and then to propose the following interventions to fix moral evil:

1. Demand submission
2. Bestow favor
3. Authorize death
4. Require faith

5. Attach guilt
6. Prescribe rules
7. Administer punishment
8. Grant pardon
9. Send to hell
10. Bring to heaven

The truth is that every action attacked here not only aligns with God's essential character but also follows naturally, even inevitably, from it. Take just five foundational doctrines, which the atheist, though not holding to them as fact, would nonetheless see no problem with their morality:

1. God alone is all-loving.
2. God alone is all-knowing.
3. God alone is all-powerful.
4. God alone is all-holy.
5. Man alone of all creatures is free.

From these five fundamentals all eleven actions under dispute (eleven because this includes the initial immorality of God's permitting moral evil in the first place) are naturally derived:

Man's Freedom ⇒ Moral Evil
God's Love + Man's Freedom ⇒ Favor
God's Knowledge + Man's Limited Knowledge ⇒ Faith
God's Power + Man's Limited Power ⇒ Submission
God's Holiness + Man's Limited Holiness ⇒ Rules
Rules + Moral Evil ⇒ Guilt
Faith + Moral Evil ⇒ Death (i.e., exile from Eden)
Guilt + Death ⇒ Punishment
Punishment + Favor ⇒ Pardon
Pardon + Freedom ⇒ Heaven and Hell
⇒ means "leads to"

The atheist might still question the morality of certain details (e.g., the extent of hell's punishments, the innocence of certain Canaanites under punishment, etc.), but it must be admitted that broadly these actions flow naturally from a moral God as described in the five doctrines listed above. It is simply not true that these interventions belong in a societal but not a divine context. They are not only appropriate coming from a moral God but they flow naturally, even necessarily, from a moral God.

Objection 5: These Interventions Are Too Restricting Coming from a God of Love

These types of interventions end up being necessary on a societal level, and no one can call immoral that which is necessary. But the Christian God claims to be a God of love. You cannot truly love someone and then impose all these types of restrictions on them. God should be able to come up with a way to fix moral evil that is far less restricting. An infinitely loving God would not want to resort to such restricting methods.

Response to Objection 5

Are these interventions really so restricting? The atheist who says God ought to fix the problem of moral evil is clearly asking for more interventions than God has already given. In other words, the atheist is requesting A- or B-level interventions, whereas these "restricting" interventions in question are merely C-level interventions. As we saw in the response to the previous objection, these interventions are not forced by a cantankerous God but instead flow naturally from a moral God. Coming from a God who is infinitely loving, knowledgeable, powerful, and holy, these interventions are simply not problematic; if there remains a problem, then it must somehow be with there being a God who is infinitely loving, knowledgeable, powerful, and holy.

There is, however, yet another reason that the accusation of restrictiveness is unfair, when it is made plain just what the atheist is forbidding God to do. Before viewing these creature-to-Creator commandments, recall that these are God-in-the-Dock (GITD) arguments. God is being placed on trial for having contradicted his own perfect nature. Thus the indictment must reckon with the entirety of the Christian system. If, for example, God did not exist, then of course these interventions might seem a bit silly or even immoral. However, note that the atheists construct their argument this way: "If God were truly moral, he wouldn't . . ." The prior assumption is that he *does* exist and that the action compromises his morality so that his existence as the most moral being is called into question. It is unfair to attack God's interventions while caricaturing them in an absurd way as if God did not exist. If God really exists, would not the following commandments seem absurdly restricting?

1. You shall not produce in your creatures feelings of inferiority (against submission).
2. You shall not produce a religion in which adherents feel special (against favor).
3. You shall not withhold immortality from your creatures (against death).
4. You shall not withhold any knowledge from your creatures (against faith).
5. You shall not make your creatures feel guilty for disobeying your commandments (against guilt).
6. You shall not prescribe any commandments your creatures feel to be unnecessary or restricting (against rules).
7. You shall not make any creature serve punishment for his crimes (against punishment).
8. No member of the Godhead shall volunteer to take your creature's punishment for his crimes (against pardon).
9. You shall not send humanity into eternity without you (against hell).

10. You shall not bring humanity into eternity with you (against heaven).

Those are only the commandments pertaining to the interventions. Keep in mind that all the while the atheist is demanding obedience to the following commandment as well:

You shall not give your creatures moral freedom (against moral evil).

Some of the above commandments are actually logically impossible as stated. For example, to say "It is immoral of you to give us moral freedom" is to use moral freedom (a moral judgment) to negate moral freedom. Likewise, "Thou shalt not produce a religion in which adherents feel special" is impossible, for how could a religion made by God and imparted to a particular group of adherents possibly fail to make them feel special? Furthermore, how could a God in any traditional sense of the term possibly interact with creatures without producing in them feelings of inferiority?

Other statements may not be self-refuting, but they definitely seem far too stringent. For example, to command the removal of faith is to essentially demand omniscience, while to command the removal of death is to demand immortality, both of which are demands for a share in divinity. The commandment against commandments amounts to a creature commanding the Creator not to give him commandments he does not like. How ironic! Or take the commandment against guilt; presumably the point of this is to heap guilt upon God for disobeying our commandment not to heap guilt upon us for disobeying his commandments (which, of course, disobey our commandment against his commandments).

All this should at least introduce into the discussion a little humility. If the atheist is considering the possibility that God exists and is measuring his actions by his supposed goodness and power, surely there should be a measure of humility recognizing that if such a God exists, he might possibly do things a bit differently than the atheist would have done. The above demands seem to hold God down in an absurdly subordinate posture, while stretching human authority well beyond its boundaries, a stretch that merely a touch of humility should break. Perhaps God is not as restrictive toward atheists as atheists are toward God. And the atheist thinks God is hard to please!

In Summary

Thus the atheist has dealt significant blows against his own arguments. Holding and accepting contradictory beliefs simultaneously, the atheist is guilty of doublethink. First, we saw that God should fix the problem of moral evil, yet in so doing he should not touch anything. Ever the zealot for human autonomy, the atheist demands freedom from the very interventions the Christian God proposes to fix the problem of moral evil. Second, we saw that the interventions the Christian God proposes in order to fix moral evil are considered immoral by the atheist but are not in themselves immoral. On the societal level, these very types of interventions are said to be necessary and thus not immoral in the least. Therefore, we find that the first inconsistency overturns the argument appealing to the problem of moral evil. Likewise, until the atheist can mount a plausible rationale behind his double standard, the second inconsistency overturns the argument appealing to the problem of divine intervention. The thinking atheist should reconsider the contradictory and impossible demands he makes of God and demand of himself a resolution of these inconsistencies.

10

The Request

As we have seen, the atheist's position is a fascinating one. Simultaneously, he holds that evil needs divine interventions and yet that divine interventions are evil. All the while, these very types of interventions are absolved on the societal level. So, on the one hand, the atheist makes clear that the interventions are not evil in themselves. Yet when from God, these interventions threaten the atheist. Because the atheist values human autonomy, though he opposes moral evil, he does not oppose the freedom that enables moral evil. As we saw in chapter 3, the atheist is not anti-freedom in the least. So, on the other hand, the atheist makes clear that freedom is not evil in itself. In the end, the atheist is against neither freedom nor the interventions, though he condemns God for employing both.

So what is the problem with freedom and with the interventions if they are not evil in themselves? If the problem is only added when God employs them, then the problem must somehow relate to God. In some sense, he cannot *fix* the problem because he *is* the problem. One would hardly expect an atheist to claim outright that the problem with God is God because this sounds like circular and emotive reasoning. However, God could be said to be the problem if the problem lies in what *kind* of God we are talking about, for atheists' writings make it clear that certain kinds of gods are more problematic than others.

After all, the name *God* can have quite different connotations. To some, the phrase *sleep like a baby* conjures pictures of peaceful, deep, uninterruptible sleep. But anyone who actually has a baby in the house could easily take the same phrase to mean bed-wetting and waking up every hour. In the same way, the phrase *run like the wind* allegedly means to run really fast and unyieldingly. However, if I am told I ought to run like the wind, I am reminded that wind is actually rather intermittent—after blowing a couple seconds, it will likely die down and then resume later when it is good and ready. Likewise, a pantheist can speak of *God*, even of *God the Father*, and even cite a Bible verse, and still be light years away from the God of the Bible. It is fascinating that even a tiny three-letter word can have multiple, even contradictory, meanings. It is kind of like the three-letter word *had*; notice how this simple word can take on different meanings:

Mary *had* a little lamb, and it tasted like chicken.

Mary *had* a little lamb sent to the butcher.

Mary *had* a little lamb, but it died.

Mary *had* a little lamb, and the doctor fainted.

Likewise, the name *God* in one sense can invoke tremendous irritation, while another kind of God would not send the most skittish squirrel into hiding.

So what kinds of gods are less problematic than the God of Christianity? One type would be the abstract divinity of pantheism, which C. S. Lewis calls a "featureless generality."[1] Christopher Hitchens contrasts a "religious" God with the far less disagreeable pantheistic divinity: "If there is a pervasive, preexisting cosmic deity, who is part of what he creates, then there is no space left for a god who intervenes in human affairs, let alone for a god who takes sides in vicious hamlet-wars between different tribes of Jews and Arabs. No text can have been written or inspired by him, for one thing, or can be the special property of one sect or tribe."[2] Another type of less problematic god would be the god of deism. Recall that on Richard Dawkins's scale, "Compared with the Old Testament's psychotic delinquent, the deist God of the eighteenth-century Enlightenment is an altogether grander being: worthy of his cosmic creation, loftily unconcerned with human affairs, sublimely aloof from our private thoughts and hopes, caring nothing for our messy sins or mumbled contritions."[3]

In other words, there is nothing too problematic with a god who is so immanent as to be part of us (pantheism) or a god who is so transcendent as to be inconsequential to us (deism). Such gods will, in the words of Lewis, "never interfere with you like that troublesome God we learned about when we were children." Instead, it is "a sort of tame God. You can switch it on when you want, but it will not bother you. All the thrills of religion and none of the cost."[4] On the other hand, there is the type of God who distinguishes himself from us yet concerns himself all the more with us. Lewis explains,

> Speak about beauty, truth and goodness, or about a God who is simply the indwelling principle of these three, speak about a great spiritual force pervading all things, a common mind of which we are all parts, a pool of generalized spirituality to which we can all flow, and you will command friendly interest. But the temperature drops as soon as you mention a God who has purposes and performs particular actions, who does one thing and not another, a concrete, choosing, commanding, prohibiting God with a determinate character. People become embarrassed or angry.[5]

Now we are getting somewhere, for it is not at all difficult to see what it is about such a God that turns otherwise pleasant things distasteful. When a concrete, personal God takes the helm, mere submission sinks into worship. Favor boomerangs into gratitude. Death transforms from the finish line of a few decades to the threshold of eternity. Faith sobers from tentative confidence to total commitment. Guilt becomes repentance. Rules become commandments. Mere punishment swells into judgment. Detached pardon descends to in-the-flesh redemption. While hell rages into the great divorce, heaven climaxes into the wedding of the Lamb. The problem of moral evil hardens into rebellion. In the end, each life becomes a battleground of eternal possibility.

Of course, not everyone would see the changes as being for the worse. Apparently, the Christian God sees the transformations as improvements. The mundane becomes the adventurous, the shadows solidify into reality, and Pinocchio toys turn into flesh-and-blood boys. From the Christian perspective, God makes everything he touches more real. It is as in Lewis's imagined bus ride from hell to heaven, where one tourist noted, "Walking proved difficult. The grass, hard as diamonds to my unsubstantial feet, made me feel as if I were walking on wrinkled rock."[6] Regardless of whether the changes prove better or worse, one observation about the changes is agreed on by both sides: A concrete, personal God makes things he touches more *risky*. The stakes are raised to the heavens.

Thus, as we have seen, the atheist's problem is with the kind of risking God who would unleash and then redeem humanity. Such a God is unsafe. God ought to have conducted a more controlled experiment. We ought to have been remedied before having to be remedied. If humanity could have been made less extreme, God would not have had to go to such extremes to reform them. He ought to have reduced the risk. After all, recall what it is the atheist expects God to do: Give us freedom, but not so much that we would abuse it. Give us rules, but only the kind we would have come up with ourselves. Forgive us our debts, but in such a way that no sacrifice is demanded of the forgiver and no indictment laid on the forgiven. The God of their wishes remedies people without repentance, approves earthly but not eternal utopias, and reveals himself without the threat of relationship. In other words, the intensity is toned down; the risk is neutralized. The thriller is mellowed into *Dick and Jane*. The villains and heroes of Gotham City are banished so that all becomes as unexceptional as Mayberry.

In Aldous Huxley's dystopian *Brave New World*, civilization has been factory conditioned and entertainment drugged into a stupor of puerile equilibrium. A fraction of the people still live on "reservations," however, and one of these "savages," named John, is brought into civilization as a sort of celebrity. In a conversation between John and a governmental executive named Mustapha Mond, we experience a clash of the risky and the controlled. John says,

"But I like the inconveniences."

"We don't. We prefer to do things comfortably."

"But I don't want comfort. I want God, I want poetry, I want real danger, I want freedom, I want goodness. I want sin."

"In fact, you're claiming the right to be unhappy."

"All right then, I'm claiming the right to be unhappy."

"Not to mention the right to grow old and ugly and impotent; the right to have syphilis and cancer; the right to have too little to eat; the right to be lousy; the right to live in constant apprehension of what may happen tomorrow; the right to catch typhoid; the right to be tortured by unspeakable pains of every kind."

"I claim them all."[7]

To this, Mustapha Mond gives a shrug of the shoulders and mutters, "You're welcome."

So perhaps the atheist is not asking God for a brave new world but a tame new world. The conspicuity of divine majesty, the enormity of eternity, the infamy of the cross, the atrocities of moral freedom—the cost of God's system and solution is simply too high. After recounting the utter horrors unleashed under heaven by moral freedom, Fyodor Dostoyevsky's Ivan Karamazov, an atheist, makes it clear to his Christian brother, Alyosha, that no amount of divine restitution can ever compensate:

> I don't want harmony. From love for humanity I don't want it. I would rather be left with the unavenged suffering. I would rather remain with my unavenged suffering and unsatisfied indignation, even if I were wrong. Besides, too high a price is asked for harmony; it's beyond our means to pay so much to enter on it. And so I hasten to give back my entrance ticket, and if I am an honest man I am bound to give it back as soon as possible. And that I am doing. It's not God that I don't accept, Alyosha, only I most respectfully return Him the ticket.[8]

What makes the cost so unbearably high? Ivan poses a hypothetical to Alyosha:

> "Imagine that you are creating a fabric of human destiny with the object of making men happy in the end, giving them peace and rest at last, but that it was essential and inevitable to torture to death only one tiny creature—that baby beating its breast with its fist, for instance—and to found that edifice on its unavenged tears, would you consent to be the architect on those conditions? Tell me, and tell the truth."
>
> "No, I wouldn't consent," said Alyosha softly.[9]

God did create a "fabric of human destiny with the object of making men happy in the end," yet founded it on tremendous risk that authorized unspeakable suffering. Does that make him therefore unloving? Disregarding the mountain of indictments he would run into, God set up a system of freedom that would unleash hardship and proposed interventions that would demand hardship. Is this not the opposite of love? On the contrary, this can only be called unloving if we are watering down the definition of love. Lewis explains,

> You asked for a loving God: you have one. The great spirit you so lightly invoked, the "lord of terrible aspect," is present: not a senile benevolence that drowsily wishes you to be happy in your own way, not the cold philanthropy of a conscientious magistrate, nor the care of a host who feels responsible for the comfort of his guests, but the consuming fire himself, the Love that made the worlds, persistent as the artist's love for his work and despotic as a man's love for a dog, provident and venerable as a father's love for a child, jealous, inexorable, exacting as love between the sexes. How this should be, I do not know: it passes reason to explain why any creatures, not to say creatures such as we, should have a value so prodigious in their Creator's eyes. It is certainly a burden of glory not only beyond our deserts but also, except in rare moments of grace, beyond our desiring.[10]

Such a weight certainly exceeds what the atheist is comfortable hauling. Whether it is called love or risk or whatever, God has set up a system that permits a tremendous amount of evil and requires a tremendous amount of striving to undo that evil. On behalf of humanity, the atheist desires to simply be rid of the troubles that such a God lets loose. Trying to convert John the Savage to the new world, Mustapha Mond assures him that civilization is far preferable without the hassles inherent in a fully human humanity. Temptation, adversity, warfare, hard moral training—the new world had gotten rid of these and had thus stabilized humanity. Recalling Shakespeare's *Hamlet*, John retorts,

> You got rid of them. Yes, that's just like you. Getting rid of everything unpleasant instead of learning to put up with it. Whether 'tis better in the mind to suffer the slings and arrows of outrageous fortune, or to take arms against a sea of troubles and by opposing end them. . . . But you don't do either. Neither suffer nor oppose. You just abolish the slings and arrows. It's too easy.[11]

Likewise, the atheist demands freedom from both suffering and opposing. God is immoral to make us suffer the instability of freedom and immoral to goad us to oppose its abuses. "Fix everything, but don't touch anything." It is no wonder Mond's official title is that of "Controller." Oh how much easier God could have made things by toning down the risk!

And the Christian agrees. God could have made things far easier—primarily on himself. In his bitterness, Ivan Karamazov had only seen half the picture. All he saw was his own love for humanity and God's alleged indifference. However, in the end, God's plan, as Architect, was to have himself tortured to death; that was the edifice on which all else was to be built. As Alyosha put it to Ivan,

> You said just now, is there a being in the whole world who would have the right to forgive and could forgive? But there is a Being and He can forgive everything, all and for all, because He gave His innocent blood for all and everything. You have forgotten Him, and on Him is built the edifice, and it is to Him they cry aloud, "Thou art just, O Lord, for Thy ways are revealed!"[12]

Apparently God had calculated the risk and determined that love was worth it. Whatever the cost to humanity, he offered to pay it. And pay it he did.

And yet, ultimately, it is the atheist who claims to be the truly courageous one, whereas God is the bully, the tyrant, the control freak. The atheist wants to be perceived as the fearless frontiersman, one foot on the cliff's edge, staring down whatever is out there. The atheist wants it straight, uncensored, undomesticated. As Dawkins boasts, "Being an atheist is nothing to be apologetic about. On the contrary, it is something to be proud of, standing tall to face the far horizon."[13] Dan Barker recalls the day that "I had truly shed the cocoon and I was, for the first time in my life, that 'new creature' of which the bible so ignorantly speaks. I had at last graduated from the childish need to look outside myself to decide who I was as a person."[14]

So the atheist claims to be unafraid, eager to discover whatever lies outside the boundaries of knowledge. Then why does the atheist insist on *reducing* everything to what can fit under his microscope? "Well, that's just where the evidence leads." Nonsense! Scientism is the starting point, the chosen epistemology that loads the premises from the outset. Scientism, the belief that all meaningful truth is scientific, though not itself a scientific statement, is nonetheless a safe one. Atheist professor Thomas Nagel admits, "I want atheism to be true and am made uneasy by the fact that some of the most intelligent and well-informed people I know are religious believers. It isn't just that I don't believe in God and, naturally, hope that I'm right in my belief. It's that I hope there is no God! I don't want there to be a God; I don't want the universe to be like that."[15] He suspects he is not alone; in fact, he says, "My guess is that this cosmic authority problem is not a rare condition and that it is responsible for much of the scientism and reductionism of our time."[16] In other words, only when the atheist at last exorcises all spirits out of the world can he relax and take on his fearless swagger. Turn our bullets into popcorn and our souls into instinct. Untie all tethers so there are no heavens hovering above or menacing hells below.

So what does this request for a more controlled universe amount to? If neither freedom nor the interventions are immoral in themselves, then what is the atheist really asking for? To answer, recall on what level all of these "immoralities" are absolved—on the *societal* level. Even if humanity employs the very same interventions, humanity will not receive the same denunciations. Why not? In the end, an enlightened humanity is capable of choosing what is best for humanity. But what are truly unpalatable to the atheist are the God-sized interventions from an uncontrollable God. On behalf of humanity, the atheist must reject divine interference outside of humanity's control. On a societal level, these interventions can still be employed in a way that honors human autonomy. On the divine level, however, humans become the object of degrading interventions rather than the interveners.

Submission and favor, death and faith, guilt and rules, punishment and pardon, hell and heaven—put them back in the hands of the people. While the gift of freedom from the hand of God is an immorality, freedom from the control of God is a truly welcome gift. Whereas the former spirals out of control, the latter is control. True, by requesting a less dangerous humanity (i.e., fix everything) and a less smothering God (i.e., don't touch anything), the atheist is asking for a more under-control existence. Yet while asking for a more under-control existence, the atheist is really asking for one that is under *human* control.

Agnostic astronomer Robert Jastrow in his book *God and the Astronomers* wondered at the puzzling reactions of his fellow scientists to the evidence for a beginning point of the universe. From these objective seekers of truth, Jastrow sensed an unmistakable mood of irritation at what should have been prized as the latest triumph of scientific discovery. Why did scientific reactions to scientific discovery sound like complaints? Einstein concluded, "This circumstance irritates me."[17] Arthur Eddington wrote, "The notion of a beginning is repugnant to me. . . . It leaves me cold."[18] Others voiced their frustrations: "I find it hard to accept the Big Bang theory; I would like to reject it." "It is such a strange conclusion. . . . It cannot really be true."[19] Jastrow concludes,

> There is a strange ring of feeling and emotion in these reactions. They come from the heart, whereas you would expect the judgments to come from the brain. Why? I think part of the answer is that scientists cannot bear the thought of a natural phenomenon which cannot be explained, even with unlimited time and money. There is a kind of religion in science; it is the religion of a person who believes there is order and harmony in the Universe, and every

event can be explained in a rational way as the product of some previous event; every effect must have its cause; there is no First Cause. Einstein wrote, "The scientist is possessed by the sense of universal causation."

This religious faith of the scientist is violated by the discovery that the world had a beginning under conditions in which the known laws of physics are not valid, and as a product of forces or circumstances we cannot discover. When that happens, the scientist has lost control.[20]

When humanity loses control, humanity feels that a longstanding arrangement has been overturned. The ancient transaction had scored a definitive triumph for human autonomy: "[T]hey exchanged the truth about God for a lie and worshiped and served the creature rather than the Creator, who is blessed forever" (Rom. 1:25). The master salesman had assured them, "You will not surely die. For God knows that when you eat of it your eyes will be opened, and you will be like God, knowing good and evil" (Gen. 3:4b–5). Ever since, any attempt of God to reconcile with his estranged creation is rejected as cheating humanity out of its most precious commodity—namely, control. So it is no surprise when irritation follows where control is lost. We prefer a user-friendly God—one that purrs when we pet him. In short, we prefer a God we can control, not a God who is in control. It is as Friedrich Nietzsche put it: "Hubris is our stance toward God, that is to say toward some alleged spider of purpose and morality behind the great snare-web of causality."[21] It turns out the real problem is with a God big enough to assume control.

Is there a name for this human hunger to retain control? Bertrand Russell wrote, "For in all things it is well to exalt the dignity of Man, by freeing him as far as possible from the tyranny of non-human Power."[22] The exaltation of man seems benign enough, and so it is. Yet the pesky theologian insists on inserting a word to tarnish its elegance. Augustine added to *exaltation* the word *inordinate*. Speaking of Adam and Eve, he wrote,

Their bad deed could not have been done had not bad will preceded it; what is more, the root of their bad will was nothing else than pride. For, "pride is the beginning of all sin." And what is pride but an appetite for inordinate exaltation? Now, exaltation is inordinate when the soul cuts itself off from the very Source [God] to which it should keep close and somehow makes itself and becomes an end to itself. This takes place when the soul becomes inordinately pleased with itself, and such self-pleasing occurs when the soul falls away from the unchangeable Good which ought to please the soul far more than the soul can please itself.[23]

The Christian calls this lust for control *pride*. The atheist who demands that God intervene and yet not intervene, all the while absolving these divine "immoralities" when under human control, is clearly exalting the creature over the Creator. Such an exaltation betrays a metaphysical impossibility and thus cannot escape being labeled "inordinate." Like any conscientious CEO, the atheist wants no surprises; the problem is that he is trying to be CEO of too enormous an enterprise. G. K. Chesterton contrasts such a temperament with that of a poet: "The poet only asks to get his head into the heavens. It is the logician who seeks to get the heavens into his head."[24] The problem for the latter can be summed up, "What a little heaven you must inhabit, with angels no bigger than butterflies!"[25]

If pride were only absurd, it might not warrant much mention. While writing on what type of character Christian leaders ought to have, the apostle Paul warned not to allow someone to rise too quickly to leadership, lest one become "puffed up with conceit and fall into the condemnation of the devil" (1 Tim. 3:6). Lewis articulates the implication: "It was through Pride that the devil became the devil."[26] Now the atheist may laugh, "Well, that might be something to consider if there were such things as devils or if God were actually petty enough to care about such trivialities as human pride." Recall what it is, however, that seems most to bring the atheist into his fiercest sobriety. The problem of moral evil is admittedly what helps make atheists into atheists. Apparently, moral evil is a problem. Christianity is clear: if you really despise the problem of moral evil, then, to be consistent and effective, you must despise pride. So anyone who claims to be serious about wanting the problem of moral evil to be remedied ought to start there.

But if the atheist desires to exalt humanity, even if inordinately, do his arguments actually achieve this? The atheist wants God to fix the problem of moral evil and yet refrain from the very interventions that would go to repair us. What he is asking of God is, of course, a contradiction. However, when it comes to what the atheist desires for *humanity*, there is not necessarily a contradiction between the two statements. In challenging God to remedy the problem of moral evil, the atheist is asking for less freedom for humanity. In imploring God to leave us alone and stop trying to remedy our immorality with his interventions, the atheist is asking for less "hard moral training," in the words of Mustapha Mond.[27] Whereas it is a contradiction to call it immoral that God does not fix moral evil and likewise immoral that he intervenes to fix moral evil, it is no contradiction to wish for less freedom and less hard moral training. After all, there is already something existing that is endowed with less freedom and bothered by less hard moral training than humanity—namely, *animals*. The more animalistic one becomes, the less freedom he can abuse and the less instruction in virtue he can effectively undergo. In short, the atheist asks, though perhaps unwittingly, for dehumanization. And here we find yet another example of doublethink: All the while believing himself to be *asserting* humanity, the atheist ends up *abolishing* humanity instead. However, God wants something far more glorious for humanity:

> See what kind of love the Father has given to us, that we should be called children of God; and so we are. (1 John 3:1a)

Bibliography

Abbagnano, Nicola. "Positivism." Translated by Nino Langiulli. In *Encyclopedia of Philosophy*, edited by Paul Edwards, vol. 6, 414–19. New York: Collier MacMillan, 1967.

Anderson, Elizabeth. "If God Is Dead, Is Everything Permitted?" In *The Portable Atheist: Essential Readings for the Nonbeliever*, edited by Christopher Hitchens, 333–48. Philadelphia: Da Capo Press, 2007.

Atkins, Peter. "Peter Atkins' Opening and Closing Statements for the Craig-Atkins Debate." *The Secular Outpost*. November 6, 2011. Accessed September 27, 2013. http://www.patheos.com/blogs/secularoutpost/2011/11/06/peter-atkins-opening-and-closing-statements-for-the-craig-atkins-debate-2011/.

Augustine. *City of God*. Translated by Gerald G. Walsh et al. Edited by Vernon J. Bourke. Garden City, NY: Doubleday, 1958.

Barker, Dan. "Foreword." In *The Christian Delusion: Why Faith Fails*, edited by John W. Loftus, 9–13. Amherst, NY: Prometheus, 2010.

——. *Godless*. Berkeley: Ulysses Press, 2008.

Boswell, James. "An Account of My Last Interview with David Hume, Esq., 3 March 1777." In *The Portable Atheist: Essential Readings for the Nonbeliever*, edited by Christopher Hitchens, 46–49. Philadelphia: Da Capo Press, 2007.

Brinton, Crane. "Enlightenment." In *Encyclopedia of Philosophy*, edited by Paul Edwards, vol. 2, 519–25. New York: Collier MacMillan, 1967.

Camus, Albert. *The Fall*. Translated by Justin O'Brien. New York: Vintage Books, 1991.

———. *The Plague*. Translated by Stuart Gilbert. New York: Alfred A. Knopf, 1948.

Carrier, Richard. "Why I Am Not a Christian." 2006. *Internet Infidels*. Accessed June 12, 2012. http://www.infidels.org/library/modern/richard _carrier/whynotchristian.html#inertgod.

Chesterton, G. K. *Orthodoxy*. 1908. Reprint, Colorado Springs: WaterBrook, 2001.

Cohen, Chapman. "Monism and Religion." In *The Portable Atheist: Essential Readings for the Nonbeliever*, edited by Christopher Hitchens, 170–77. Philadelphia: Da Capo Press, 2007.

Darwin, Charles. *The Autobiography of Charles Darwin: 1809–1882*. Edited by Nora Barlow. New York: The Norton Library, 1958.

Dawkins, Richard. *The God Delusion*. Boston: Mariner, 2008.

———. "Is Science a Religion?" *Humanist*, January/February 1997. Accessed September 26, 2013. http://www.thehumanist.org/humanist/articles /dawkins.html.

Dennett, Daniel C. "The Bright Stuff." *New York Times*, July 12, 2003. Accessed June 15, 2012. http://www.nytimes.com/2003/07/12/opinion/the -bright-stuff.html?pagewanted=all&src=pm.

———. "Thank Goodness." In *The Portable Atheist: Essential Readings for the Nonbeliever*, edited by Christopher Hitchens, 277–83. Philadelphia: Da Capo Press, 2007.

Detzler, Wayne. "Europe in Revolt." In *Introduction to the History of Christianity*, edited by Tim Dowley, 508–17. Minneapolis: Fortress, 2002.

Dostoyevsky, Fyodor. "From *The Brothers Karamazov*." In *The Problem of Evil: A Reader*, edited by Mark Larrimore, 277–82. Malden, MA: Blackwell, 2001.

Ehrman, Bart. *God's Problem: How the Bible Fails to Answer Our Most Important Question—Why We Suffer*. San Francisco: HarperOne, 2008.

Einstein, Albert. "Selected Writings on Religion." In *The Portable Atheist: Essential Readings for the Nonbeliever*, edited by Christopher Hitchens, 155–65. Philadelphia: Da Capo Press, 2007.

Feuerbach, Ludwig. *The Essence of Christianity*. Translated by George Eliot. New York: Harper and Brothers, 1957.

Flew, Antony, and Roy Abraham Varghese. *There Is a God: How the World's Most Notorious Atheist Changed His Mind*. San Francisco: HarperOne, 2007.

Freud, Sigmund. "From *The Future of an Illusion*." In *The Portable Atheist: Essential Readings for the Nonbeliever*, edited by Christopher Hitchens, 147–54. Philadelphia: Da Capo Press, 2007.

———. *The Future of an Illusion*. Edited by Todd Dufresne. Translated by Gregory C. Richter. Peterborough, ON: Broadview Press, 2012.

Geisler, Norman L., and Frank Turek. *I Don't Have Enough Faith to Be an Atheist*. Wheaton: Crossway, 2004.

Goldman, Emma. "The Philosophy of Atheism." In *The Portable Atheist: Essential Readings for the Nonbeliever*, edited by Christopher Hitchens, 129–33. Philadelphia: Da Capo Press, 2007.

Guinness, Os. *Unspeakable: Facing Up to the Challenge of Evil*. San Francisco: HarperSanFrancisco, 2005.

Harris, Sam. *The End of Faith: Religion, Terror, and the Future of Reason*. New York: Norton, 2004.

———. *Letter to a Christian Nation*. New York: Vintage Books, 2008.

———. *The Moral Landscape: How Science Can Determine Human Values*. New York: Free Press, 2010.

Henke, James. *Lennon Legend: An Illustrated Life of John Lennon*. San Francisco: Chronicle Books, 2003.

Hepburn, R. W. "Autonomy and Heteronomy." In *The Oxford Companion to Philosophy*. 2nd ed. Edited by Ted Honderich. Oxford: Oxford University Press, 2005.

Hick, John. "Reincarnation and the Meaning of Life." *John Hick: The Official Website*. Accessed November 9, 2013. http://www.johnhick.org.uk/jsite/index.php?option=com_content&view=article&id=54:rein&catid=37:articles&Itemid=58.

Hitchens, Christopher. *God Is Not Great: How Religion Poisons Everything*. New York: Twelve, 2007.

———. "Introduction." In *The Portable Atheist: Essential Readings for the Nonbeliever*, edited by Christopher Hitchens, xiii–xxvi. Philadelphia: Da Capo Press, 2007.

Hitchens, Peter. *The Rage against God: How Atheism Led Me to Faith*. Grand Rapids: Zondervan, 2010.

Hume, David. "Dialogues Concerning Natural Religion." In *The Problem of Evil: A Reader*, edited by Mark Larrimore, 216–23. Malden, MA: Blackwell, 2001.

———. "The Natural History of Religion." In *The Portable Atheist: Essential Readings for the Nonbeliever*, edited by Christopher Hitchens, 26–32. Philadelphia: Da Capo Press, 2007.

Huxley, Aldous. *Brave New World and Brave New World Revisited*. New York: Harper Perennial Modern Classics, 2005.

Jastrow, Robert. *God and the Astronomers*. 2nd ed. Toronto: George J. McLeod, 1992.

Jefferson, Thomas. *Memoir, Correspondence, and Miscellanies from the Papers of Thomas Jefferson*, edited by Thomas Jefferson Randolph, vol. 3. Charlottesville, VA: F. Carr, 1829.

Jillette, Penn. "There Is No God." In *The Portable Atheist: Essential Readings for the Nonbeliever*, edited by Christopher Hitchens, 349–50. Philadelphia: Da Capo Press, 2007.

Kaufmann, Walter. *Critique of Religion and Philosophy*. Princeton: Princeton University Press, 1990.

Kurtz, Paul, ed. *Humanist Manifestos I and II*. Buffalo: Prometheus, 1973.

———. *Humanist Manifesto 2000: A Call for a New Planetary Humanism*. Amherst, NY: Prometheus, 2000.

Lewis, C. S. "God in the Dock." In *God in the Dock: Essays on Theology and Ethics*, edited by Walter Hooper, 240–44. Grand Rapids: Eerdmans, 1970.

———. *The Great Divorce*. San Francisco: HarperSanFrancisco, 2001.

———. *Mere Christianity*. New York: HarperCollins, 2001.

———. *Miracles*. San Francisco: HarperSanFrancisco, 2001.

———. *The Problem of Pain*. San Francisco: HarperSanFrancisco, 2001.

Loftus, John W. "The Darwinian Problem of Evil." In *The Christian Delusion: Why Faith Fails*, edited by John W. Loftus, 237–70. Amherst, NY: Prometheus, 2009.

———. "What We've Got Here Is a Failure to Communicate." In *The Christian Delusion: Why Faith Fails*, edited by John W. Loftus, 181–206. Amherst, NY: Prometheus, 2009.

Lucretius. "De Rerum Natura (On the Nature of Things)." Translated by W. Hannaford Brown. In *The Portable Atheist: Essential Readings for the Nonbeliever*, edited by Christopher Hitchens, 1–6. Philadelphia: Da Capo Press, 2007.

Marx, Karl. "Contribution to the Critique of Hegel's Philosophy of Right." In *The Portable Atheist: Essential Readings for the Nonbeliever*, edited by Christopher Hitchens, 64–74. Philadelphia: Da Capo Press, 2007.

McEwan, Ian. "End of the World Blues." In *The Portable Atheist: Essential Readings for the Nonbeliever*, edited by Christopher Hitchens, 351–65. Philadelphia: Da Capo Press, 2007.

Nagel, Thomas. *The Last Word*. Oxford: Oxford University Press, 1997.

Nietzsche, Friedrich. *The Antichrist*. Translated by H. L. Mencken. New York: Alfred A. Knopf, 1920.

———. "From *The Gay Science*." In *The Portable Nietzsche*, edited by Walter Kaufmann, 93–101. New York: Viking, 1968.

———. *On the Genealogy of Morality: A Polemic*. Translated by Maudemarie Clark and Alan J. Swensen. Indianapolis: Hackett, 1998.

———. *Thus Spake Zarathustra*. Translated by Walter Kaufmann. New York: Penguin, 1982.

Onfray, Michel. *Atheist Manifesto: The Case against Christianity, Judaism, and Islam*. Translated by Jeremy Leggatt. New York: Arcade, 2011.

Orwell, George. *Nineteen Eighty-Four*. Fairfield, IA: First World Library Literary Society, 2004.

Paine, Thomas. *The Age of Reason: Being an Investigation of True and Fabulous Theology*. Edited by Moncure Daniel Conway. New York: Truth Seeker, 1898.

Palmer, Michael. "Paul Tillich's Theology of Culture." In *Paul Tillich: Main Works*, vol. 2, *Writings in the Philosophy of Culture*, edited by Michael Palmer, 1–31. Berlin: de Gruyter, 1990.

Parsons, Keith. "Hell: Christianity's Most Damnable Doctrine." In *The End of Christianity*, edited by John W. Loftus, 233–54. Amherst, NY: Prometheus, 2011.

Pascal, Blaise. *Pascal's Pensées*. Middlesex, UK: The Echo Library, 2008.

Pulliam, Ken. "The Absurdity of the Atonement." In *The End of Christianity*, edited by John W. Loftus, 281–94. Amherst, NY: Prometheus, 2011.

Quinn, Philip L. "Philosophy of Religion." In *The Cambridge Dictionary of Philosophy*, 2nd ed., edited by Robert Audi, 696–700. Cambridge: Cambridge University Press, 2006.

Rowe, William L. "The Problem of Evil and Some Varieties of Atheism." In *The Problem of Evil*, edited by Marilyn McCord Adams and Robert Merrihew Adams, 126–37. Oxford: Oxford University Press, 1996.

Rushdie, Salman. "Imagine There's No Heaven: A Letter to the Six Billionth World Citizen." In *The Portable Atheist: Essential Readings for the Nonbeliever*, edited by Christopher Hitchens, 380–83. Philadelphia: Da Capo Press, 2007.

Russell, Bertrand. "Can Religion Cure Our Troubles?" In *Why I Am Not a Christian*, edited by Paul Edwards, 193–204. New York: Touchstone, 1957.

———. "Do We Survive Death?" In *Why I Am Not a Christian*, edited by Paul Edwards, 88–93. New York: Touchstone, 1957.

———. "A Free Man's Worship." In *Why I Am Not a Christian*, edited by Paul Edwards, 104–16. New York: Touchstone, 1957.

———. "Has Religion Made Useful Contributions to Civilization?" In *Why I Am Not a Christian*, edited by Paul Edwards, 24–47. New York: Touchstone, 1957.

———. *History of Western Philosophy*. London: Routledge, 2004.

———. "The New Generation." In *Why I Am Not a Christian*, edited by Paul Edwards, 157–67. New York: Touchstone, 1957.

———. "Our Sexual Ethics." In *Why I Am Not a Christian*, edited by Paul Edwards, 168–78. New York: Touchstone, 1957.

———. "An Outline of Intellectual Rubbish." In *The Portable Atheist: Essential Readings for the Nonbeliever*, edited by Christopher Hitchens, 181–206. Philadelphia: Da Capo Press, 2007.

———. "Religion and Morals." In *Why I Am Not a Christian*, edited by Paul Edwards, 205–6. New York: Touchstone, 1957.

———. "What I Believe." In *Why I Am Not a Christian*, edited by Paul Edwards, 48–87. New York: Touchstone, 1957.

———. "Why I Am Not a Christian." In *Why I Am Not a Christian*, edited by Paul Edwards, 3–23. New York: Touchstone, 1957.

Sagan, Carl. "The God Hypothesis." In *The Portable Atheist: Essential Readings for the Nonbeliever*, edited by Christopher Hitchens, 226–38. Philadelphia: Da Capo Press, 2007.

Shelley, Percy Bysshe. "A Refutation of Deism." In *The Portable Atheist: Essential Readings for the Nonbeliever*, edited by Christopher Hitchens, 50–56. Philadelphia: Da Capo Press, 2007.

Smith, George H. *Atheism: The Case against God*. Amherst, NY: Prometheus, 1979.

Spiegel, James S. *The Making of an Atheist: How Immorality Leads to Unbelief*. Chicago: Moody, 2010.

Strobel, Lee. *The Case for Faith: A Journalist Investigates the Toughest Objections to Christianity*. Grand Rapids: Zondervan, 2000.

Swinburne, Richard G. "Religion, Problems of the Philosophy of." In *The Oxford Companion to Philosophy*, 2nd ed., edited by Ted Honderich, 805–8. Oxford: Oxford University Press, 2005.

Tait, Katharine. *My Father Bertrand Russell*. Bristol, UK: Thoemmes, 1996.

Templeton, Charles. "Questions to Ask Yourself." In *The Portable Atheist: Essential Readings for the Nonbeliever*, edited by Christopher Hitchens, 285–86. Philadelphia: Da Capo Press, 2007.

Thomas, Jo. "In Oklahoma City, Silence for Each of the Victims." *New York Times*, April 20, 1996. Accessed August 9, 2012. http://www.nytimes.com/1996/04/20/us/in-oklahoma-city-silence-for-each-of-the-victims.html?pagewanted=all&src=pm.

Twain, Mark. *Mark Twain at Your Fingertips: A Book of Quotations*. Edited by Caroline Thomas Harnsberger. Mineola, NY: Dover, 2009.

———. "Thoughts of God." In *The Portable Atheist: Essential Readings for the Nonbeliever*, edited by Christopher Hitchens, 116–18. Philadelphia: Da Capo Press, 2007.

Vitz, Paul C. *Faith of the Fatherless: The Psychology of Atheism*. Dallas: Spence, 1999.

Weinberg, Steven. "What about God?" In *The Portable Atheist: Essential Readings for the Nonbeliever*, edited by Christopher Hitchens, 366–79. Philadelphia: Da Capo Press, 2007.

Weisberger, Andrea M. "The Argument from Evil." In *The Cambridge Companion to Atheism*, edited by Michael Martin, 166–81. Cambridge: Cambridge University Press, 2011.

Wilson, A. N. "Why I Believe Again." In *New Statesman*, April 2, 2009. Accessed May 5, 2012. http://www.newstatesman.com/religion/2009/04/conversion-experience-atheism.

Notes

Introduction

1. Orwell, *Nineteen Eighty-Four*, 264.
2. Lewis, "God in the Dock."
3. Swinburne, "Religion, Problems of the Philosophy of," 807.
4. Quinn, "Philosophy of Religion," 699.
5. Hepburn, "Autonomy and Heteronomy," 72.
6. Palmer, "Paul Tillich's Theology of Culture," 3.
7. Lewis, *Problem of Pain*, 24.

Chapter 1: The Problem of Moral Evil

1. Harris, *End of Faith*, 66–67.
2. Swinburne, "Religion, Problems of the Philosophy of," 807.
3. Dawkins, *God Delusion*, 89.
4. Rowe, "Problem of Evil," 129–30.
5. Russell, "Useful Contributions," 29.
6. Russell, "Outline of Intellectual Rubbish," 187.
7. Sagan, "God Hypothesis," 237.
8. Barker, *Godless*, 124; emphasis in original.
9. Ibid., 126.
10. Carrier, "Why I Am Not a Christian."
11. Smith, *Atheism*, 83.
12. Twain, "Thoughts of God," 117–18; emphasis in original.
13. Russell, "Why I Am Not a Christian," 10.
14. Hume, "Dialogues Concerning Natural Religion," 220.

15. Ibid., 218.
16. Russell, "Do We Survive Death?," 93.
17. Weisberger, "Argument from Evil," 166.
18. Thomas, "In Oklahoma City."
19. McEwan, "End of the World Blues," 365.
20. Loftus, "Darwinian Problem of Evil," 239.
21. Loftus, "What We've Got Here," 201.
22. Ehrman, *God's Problem*, 5.
23. Carrier, "Why I Am Not a Christian"; emphasis in original.
24. Weisberger, "Argument from Evil," 179.
25. Weinberg, "What about God?," 372.
26. Carrier, "Why I Am Not a Christian."
27. Harris, *Letter to a Christian Nation*, 50–51; emphasis in original.
28. Ibid., 52.
29. Harris, *End of Faith*, 173.
30. Flew and Varghese, *There Is a God*, 13–14.
31. Ehrman, *God's Problem*, 1.
32. Carrier, "Why I Am Not a Christian."
33. George Carlin, quoted in Spiegel, *Making of an Atheist*, 62.
34. Quoted in Strobel, *Case for Faith*, 14; emphasis in original.
35. Guinness, *Unspeakable*, 34.
36. Barker, *Godless*, 212.
37. Quoted in Guinness, *Unspeakable*, 37.
38. Quoted in ibid.
39. Weisberger, "Argument from Evil," 174.
40. See Guinness, *Unspeakable*, 43.
41. Hume, "Dialogues Concerning Natural Religion," 223.
42. Ibid., 218.

Chapter 2: The Value of Human Autonomy

1. Einstein, "Selected Writings on Religion," 163.
2. Barker, *Godless*, 353.
3. Feuerbach, *Essence of Christianity*, 12.
4. Freud, "From *The Future of an Illusion*," 147.
5. Goldman, "Philosophy of Atheism," 129.
6. Freud, "From *The Future of an Illusion*," 152.
7. Kurtz, *Humanist Manifesto 2000*, 26.
8. Feuerbach, *Essence of Christianity*, 13.
9. Onfray, *Atheist Manifesto*, 67.
10. Goldman, "Philosophy of Atheism," 130.
11. Feuerbach, *Essence of Christianity*, 32.
12. See Abbagnano, "Positivism," 415.

13. Detzler, "Europe in Revolt," 509.
14. Brinton, "Enlightenment," 522.
15. Onfray, *Atheist Manifesto*, 5–6.
16. Freud, "From *The Future of an Illusion*," 153.
17. Freud, *Future of an Illusion*, 169.
18. Shelley, "A Refutation of Deism," 55.
19. Dennett, "The Bright Stuff."
20. Nietzsche, *Antichrist*, 37–38.
21. Wilson, "Why I Believe Again."
22. Vitz, *Faith of the Fatherless*, 135.
23. P. Hitchens, *Rage against God*, 24.
24. Nietzsche, "From *The Gay Science*," 96.
25. Kurtz, *Humanist Manifestos I and II*, 16.
26. Geisler and Turek, *I Don't Have Enough Faith*, 20.
27. Atkins, "Opening and Closing Statements."
28. Goldman, "Philosophy of Atheism," 133.
29. Marx, "Hegel's Philosophy of Right," 70.
30. Barker, *Godless*, 42.
31. Dawkins, *God Delusion*, 403–4.
32. Barker, *Godless*, 344.
33. C. Hitchens, "Introduction," xvi.
34. Rushdie, "Imagine There's No Heaven," 383.
35. Barker, *Godless*, 355.
36. Kurtz, *Humanist Manifesto 2000*, 62–63.
37. Goldman, "Philosophy of Atheism," 130.
38. Ibid., 133.
39. Russell, "Useful Contributions," 47.
40. Lucretius, "De Rerum Natura (On the Nature of Things)," 2.
41. Dawkins, *God Delusion*, 420.
42. Ibid., 22; emphasis in original.
43. Ibid., 276.

Chapter 3: Submission and Favor

1. C. Hitchens, *God Is Not Great*, 4.
2. Feuerbach, *Essence of Christianity*, 29–30.
3. Barker, *Godless*, 166.
4. Feuerbach, *Essence of Christianity*, 27; emphasis in original.
5. C. Hitchens, *God Is Not Great*, 248.
6. Russell, "What I Believe," 74.
7. Hume, "The Natural History of Religion," 31.
8. C. Hitchens, *God Is Not Great*, 230–31.
9. Ibid., 232; emphasis in original.

10. Harris, *End of Faith*, 226.
11. Russell, "A Free Man's Worship," 112.
12. Nietzsche, *Antichrist*, 135.
13. C. Hitchens, *God Is Not Great*, 73–74.
14. Barker, *Godless*, 184.
15. Feuerbach, *Essence of Christianity*, 26.
16. Nietzsche, *Antichrist*, 154.
17. Russell, "Useful Contributions," 23.
18. Kurtz, *Humanist Manifestos I and II*, 16.
19. Ibid., 9.
20. Russell, "Outline of Intellectual Rubbish," 203.
21. Barker, *Godless*, 344.
22. Russell, "Why I Am Not a Christian," 22.
23. Kaufmann, *Critique of Religion and Philosophy*, 359.
24. Dawkins, *God Delusion*, 260.
25. C. Hitchens, *God Is Not Great*, 6.
26. Ibid., 6.
27. Goldman, "Philosophy of Atheism," 132.
28. Barker, *Godless*, 184.
29. Dennett, "Thank Goodness," 281.
30. Barker, *Godless*, 341.
31. C. Hitchens, *God Is Not Great*, 285.
32. Russell, "Useful Contributions," 42.
33. Harris, *End of Faith*, 172.
34. C. Hitchens, *God Is Not Great*, 74.
35. Nietzsche, *Antichrist*, 122–23.
36. Harris, *Letter to a Christian Nation*, 74; emphasis in original.
37. Jillette, "There Is No God," 349.
38. C. Hitchens, *God Is Not Great*, 7.
39. Harris, *Letter to a Christian Nation*, 54.
40. Russell, "Outline of Intellectual Rubbish," 189.
41. C. Hitchens, *God Is Not Great*, 76.
42. Russell, "A Free Man's Worship," 109.
43. Kurtz, *Humanist Manifesto 2000*, 62–63.
44. Camus, *Fall*, 133.
45. Dawkins, *God Delusion*, 97–98.
46. Ibid., 98; emphasis in original.
47. Russell, "A Free Man's Worship," 109.
48. Feuerbach, *Essence of Christianity*, 27.
49. Russell, "Useful Contributions," 23.
50. Barker, *Godless*, 166.
51. Russell, "Why I Am Not a Christian," 23.

52. Quoted in Dawkins, *God Delusion*, 283.
53. Tait, *My Father Bertrand Russell*, 184.
54. Pascal, *Pascal's Pensées*, 100.
55. Dennett, "Bright Stuff."

Chapter 4: Death and Faith

1. Onfray, *Atheist Manifesto*, 68.
2. C. Hitchens, *God Is Not Great*, 248.
3. Camus, *Plague*, 86–87.
4. Ibid., 205.
5. Carrier, "Why I Am Not a Christian"; emphasis in original.
6. Harris, *End of Faith*, 172.
7. Russell, "Why I Am Not a Christian," 12.
8. Camus, *Plague*, 196–97.
9. Ibid., 116.
10. Nietzsche, *Antichrist*, 148.
11. Dawkins, *God Delusion*, 232.
12. C. Hitchens, *God Is Not Great*, 71.
13. Onfray, *Atheist Manifesto*, 13.
14. Harris, *End of Faith*, 23; emphasis in original.
15. C. Hitchens, *God Is Not Great*, 12.
16. Ibid., 10–11; emphasis in original.
17. Harris, *End of Faith*, 35; emphasis in original.
18. Ibid., 45.
19. C. Hitchens, *God Is Not Great*, 32.
20. Harris, *End of Faith*, 29; emphasis in original.
21. Barker, *Godless*, 169.
22. Russell, "Our Sexual Ethics," 176–77.
23. Russell, "Useful Contributions," 28.
24. Ibid., 29.
25. Onfray, *Atheist Manifesto*, 60.
26. Russell, "Useful Contributions," 28.
27. Dawkins, "Is Science a Religion?"
28. Harris, *End of Faith*, 172.
29. C. Hitchens, *God Is Not Great*, 5–6.
30. Richard Dawkins, quoted in Spiegel, *Making of an Atheist*, 31.
31. Russell, "What I Believe," 54.
32. Russell, "Free Man's Worship," 116.
33. Boswell, "Last Interview with David Hume," 47.
34. Barker, *Godless*, 343.
35. Dawkins, *God Delusion*, 404–5.
36. Russell, "Why I Am Not a Christian," 11.

37. Russell, "Do We Survive Death?," 93.
38. Russell, "Why I Am Not a Christian," 23.
39. Kurtz, *Humanist Manifesto 2000*, 62.
40. Kurtz, *Humanist Manifestos I and II*, 14.
41. Kurtz, *Humanist Manifesto 2000*, 13.
42. Russell, "Why I Am Not a Christian," 22.
43. Cohen, "Monism and Religion," 170.
44. C. Hitchens, *God Is Not Great*, 262; emphasis in original.
45. Harris, *End of Faith*, 40.
46. Lewis, *Miracles*, 149.
47. Harris, *End of Faith*, 172.
48. Barker, *Godless*, 103.
49. Onfray, *Atheist Manifesto*, 98.

Chapter 5: Guilt and Rules

1. Nietzsche, *Antichrist*, 140–41.
2. Dawkins, *God Delusion*, 243.
3. C. Hitchens, *God Is Not Great*, 173–93.
4. Ibid., 185–86.
5. Goldman, "Philosophy of Atheism," 133.
6. Harris, *End of Faith*, 157.
7. Russell, "Useful Contributions," 41.
8. Ibid., 40.
9. Russell, "New Generation," 159.
10. Onfray, *Atheist Manifesto*, 51.
11. Barker, *Godless*, 355.
12. Ibid., 355.
13. Russell, "What I Believe," 71.
14. Feuerbach, *Essence of Christianity*, 27–28.
15. Barker, *Godless*, 171.
16. C. Hitchens, *God Is Not Great*, 7.
17. Nietzsche, *Antichrist*, 144.
18. Barker, *Godless*, 355.
19. Russell, "Religion and Morals," 205.
20. Russell, "Useful Contributions," 27.
21. C. Hitchens, *God Is Not Great*, 56.
22. Barker, *Godless*, 183.
23. Russell, "New Generation," 166.
24. Russell, "Useful Contributions," 46–47.
25. Barker, *Godless*, 355.
26. Sagan, "God Hypothesis," 237.
27. C. Hitchens, *God Is Not Great*, 214.

28. Russell, "Outline of Intellectual Rubbish," 187.
29. Russell, "Can Religion Cure Our Troubles?," 194.
30. Harris, *End of Faith*, 171–72.
31. Russell, "What I Believe," 65–66.
32. C. Hitchens, *God Is Not Great*, 27.
33. Ibid., 54.
34. Russell, "Useful Contributions," 26.
35. Harris, *Letter to a Christian Nation*, 26.
36. Dawkins, *God Delusion*, 58.
37. Ibid., 300.
38. Kurtz, *Humanist Manifestos I and II*, 18.
39. Harris, *End of Faith*, 164.
40. Russell, "What I Believe," 68.
41. C. Hitchens, *God Is Not Great*, 283.
42. Kurtz, *Humanist Manifestos I and II*, 18.
43. Kurtz, *Humanist Manifesto 2000*, 34.
44. C. Hitchens, *God Is Not Great*, 100; emphasis in original.
45. Ibid., 212; emphasis in original.
46. Barker, *Godless*, 196.
47. C. Hitchens, *God Is Not Great*, 213; emphasis in original.
48. Harris, *Letter to a Christian Nation*, 20.
49. Ibid., 8.
50. Ibid.
51. Harris, *End of Faith*, 158.
52. Ibid., 159.
53. Ibid., 171.
54. Darwin, *Autobiography*, 94.
55. Dawkins, *God Delusion*, 81.
56. C. Hitchens, *God Is Not Great*, 99.
57. Harris, *Letter to a Christian Nation*, 24–25.
58. C. Hitchens, *God Is Not Great*, 100.
59. Nietzsche, *Thus Spake Zarathustra*, 138.
60. Ibid., 139.
61. Ibid., 178.
62. Russell, *History of Western Philosophy*, 697.
63. Onfray, *Atheist Manifesto*, 69–70.
64. Dawkins, *God Delusion*, 59.
65. Ibid., 285.
66. C. Hitchens, *God Is Not Great*, 64.
67. Dawkins, *God Delusion*, 270.
68. C. Hitchens, *God Is Not Great*, 52.
69. Ibid., 211.

70. Russell, "Free Man's Worship," 112.
71. Barker, *Godless*, 202.
72. Russell, "Our Sexual Ethics," 175.
73. Russell, "Religion and Morals," 205.
74. Ibid., 205.
75. Russell, "Useful Contributions," 26.
76. Russell, "Why I Am Not a Christian," 22.

Chapter 6: Punishment and Pardon

1. Dawkins, *God Delusion*, 285.
2. Lewis, *Problem of Pain*, 50.
3. Quoted in Barker, "Foreword," 12.
4. Jefferson, *Memoir, Correspondence, and Miscellanies*, 3:326.
5. Paine, *Age of Reason*, 18.
6. Darwin, *Autobiography*, 85.
7. Harris, *End of Faith*, 173.
8. Ibid., 173.
9. Barker, *Godless*, 170.
10. Dawkins, *God Delusion*, 51.
11. Ibid., 269.
12. Barker, *Godless*, 172–73.
13. Harris, *End of Faith*, 18.
14. Onfray, *Atheist Manifesto*, 41.
15. Harris, *Letter to a Christian Nation*, 96.
16. C. Hitchens, *God Is Not Great*, 211.
17. Pulliam, "Absurdity of the Atonement," 184.
18. Ibid., 183.
19. Dawkins, *God Delusion*, 287; emphasis in original.
20. Barker, *Godless*, 202.
21. Dawkins, *God Delusion*, 286.
22. Ibid., 284.
23. Nietzsche, *Antichrist*, 117.
24. C. Hitchens, *God Is Not Great*, 17; emphasis in original.
25. Ibid., 13.
26. Ibid., 209.
27. Ibid., 211.
28. Anderson, "If God Is Dead," 339.
29. Pulliam, "Absurdity of the Atonement," 184.
30. Barker, *Godless*, 89.
31. Russell, "Outline of Intellectual Rubbish," 198.
32. Quoted in Dawkins, *God Delusion*, 89.
33. C. Hitchens, *God Is Not Great*, 56.

34. Harris, *End of Faith*, 52–53.
35. Goldman, "Philosophy of Atheism," 131–32.
36. Anderson, "If God Is Dead," 339.
37. Dawkins, *God Delusion*, 287.
38. Barker, *Godless*, 355.
39. Ibid., 59.

Chapter 7: Hell and Heaven

1. Kurtz, *Humanist Manifestos I and II*, 16.
2. John Lennon, "Imagine," quoted in Henke, *Lennon Legend*, 48.
3. Russell, "Why I Am Not a Christian," 17.
4. Barker, *Godless*, 181.
5. Ibid.
6. C. Hitchens, *God Is Not Great*, 175–76.
7. Ibid., 60.
8. Templeton, "Questions to Ask Yourself," 285; emphasis in original.
9. Smith, *Atheism*, 79.
10. Dawkins, *God Delusion*, 357–58; emphasis in original.
11. Barker, *Godless*, 183.
12. Ibid., 151.
13. Russell, "Why I Am Not a Christian," 18.
14. Parsons, "Hell," 253.
15. C. Hitchens, *God Is Not Great*, 57.
16. Ibid., 56.
17. Goldman, "Philosophy of Atheism," 131.
18. Darwin, *Autobiography*, 87.
19. Parsons, "Hell," 254.
20. C. Hitchens, *God Is Not Great*, 15–16.
21. Barker, *Godless*, 170.
22. C. Hitchens, "Introduction," xvi.
23. Barker, *Godless*, 221.
24. Hume, "Natural History of Religion," 30.
25. Dawkins, *God Delusion*, 259.
26. Barker, *Godless*, 77.
27. Twain, "Tammany and Croker," *Mark Twain's Speeches* (1910), 117, quoted in Twain, *Mark Twain at Your Fingertips*, 449.
28. Russell, "Our Sexual Ethics," 169.
29. Parsons, "Hell," 253; emphasis in original.
30. P. Hitchens, *Rage against God*, 103.
31. Ibid., 104–5.
32. Russell, "Outline of Intellectual Rubbish," 189.
33. Anderson, "If God Is Dead," 346.

34. Ibid., 347.
35. Ibid.
36. Geisler and Turek, *I Don't Have Enough Faith*, 42.
37. Onfray, *Atheist Manifesto*, 66.
38. Kurtz, *Humanist Manifestos I and II*, 10.
39. Russell, "Useful Contributions," 47.
40. Rushdie, "Imagine There's No Heaven," 383.

Chapter 8: Inconsistencies

1. Barker, *Godless*, 101.
2. Harris, *Letter to a Christian Nation*, 5.
3. Barker, *Godless*, 184.
4. C. Hitchens, *God Is Not Great*, 74.
5. Lewis, *Mere Christianity*, 74.
6. C. Hitchens, *God Is Not Great*, 5–6.
7. Barker, *Godless*, 343.
8. Onfray, *Atheist Manifesto*, 53.
9. C. Hitchens, *God Is Not Great*, 52.
10. Barker, *Godless*, 183.
11. Harris, *Letter to a Christian Nation*, 10–11.
12. Barker, *Godless*, 168.
13. C. Hitchens, *God Is Not Great*, 209.
14. Barker, *Godless*, 59.
15. Parsons, "Hell," 253; emphasis in original.
16. Dawkins, *God Delusion*, 259.
17. Lewis, *Problem of Pain*, 149.
18. Dawkins, *God Delusion*, 97.
19. Russell, "Free Man's Worship," 109.
20. Barker, *Godless*, 343.
21. Russell, "Free Man's Worship," 109.
22. C. Hitchens, *God Is Not Great*, 52.
23. Russell, "Our Sexual Ethics," 175.
24. Harris, *End of Faith*, 52–53.
25. Dawkins, *God Delusion*, 287.
26. Anderson, "If God Is Dead," 347.
27. Russell, "Useful Contributions," 47.
28. Ibid.
29. Dawkins, *God Delusion*, 120.

Chapter 9: Responses and Objections

1. Barker, *Godless*, 36.
2. Lewis, *Problem of Pain*, 18.
3. Hick, "Reincarnation."

Chapter 10: The Request

1. Lewis, *Miracles*, 145.
2. C. Hitchens, *God Is Not Great*, 262.
3. Dawkins, *God Delusion*, 59.
4. Lewis, *Mere Christianity*, 27.
5. Lewis, *Miracles*, 129–30.
6. Lewis, *Great Divorce*, 25.
7. Huxley, *Brave New World and Brave New World Revisited*, 215.
8. Dostoyevsky, "From *The Brothers Karamazov*," 281.
9. Ibid., 281–82.
10. Lewis, *Problem of Pain*, 39–40.
11. Huxley, *Brave New World and Brave New World Revisited*, 213–14.
12. Dostoyevsky, "From *The Brothers Karamazov*," 282.
13. Dawkins, *God Delusion*, 26.
14. Barker, *Godless*, 42.
15. Nagel, *Last Word*, 130.
16. Ibid., 131.
17. Jastrow, *God and the Astronomers*, 104–5.
18. Ibid.
19. Ibid.
20. Ibid., 105.
21. Nietzsche, *On the Genealogy of Morality*, 80.
22. Russell, "Free Man's Worship," 109.
23. Augustine, *City of God*, 308–9.
24. Chesterton, *Orthodoxy*, 15.
25. Ibid., 20.
26. Lewis, *Mere Christianity*, 122.
27. Huxley, *Brave New World and Brave New World Revisited*, 213.

Norman L. Geisler (BA, MA, Wheaton College; PhD, Loyola University) has authored or coauthored over eighty books and hundreds of articles. He has taught theology, philosophy, and apologetics on the college or graduate level for over fifty years. He has served as a professor at some of the finest seminaries in the United States, including Trinity Evangelical Divinity School, Dallas Theological Seminary, and Southern Evangelical Seminary. He now lends his talents to Veritas Evangelical Seminary in Murrieta, California, as the Distinguished Professor of Apologetics.

Daniel J. McCoy (MA, Veritas Evangelical Seminary) is an associate minister and Christian school teacher, and is currently working toward a PhD through North-West University.

Defending the Traditional Evangelical Teaching of Biblical Inerrancy for a New Generation

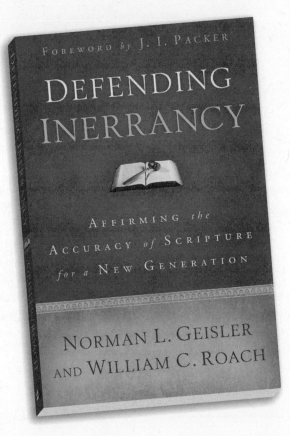

"We owe a debt to Norm Geisler and Bill Roach for their willingness to stand at the front line in this renewed battle for the Bible."
—**John MacArthur**, pastor, Grace Community Church, Sun Valley, California; president, The Master's College and Seminary

BakerBooks
Relevant. Intelligent. Engaging.

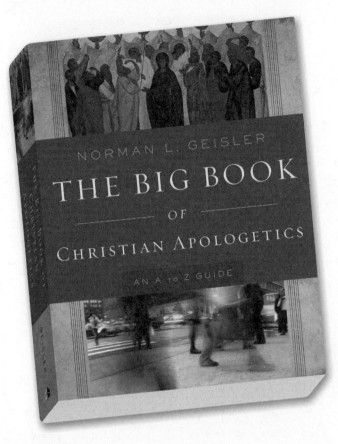

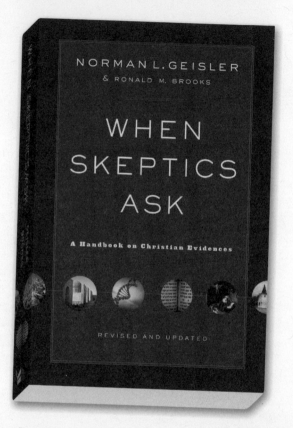